Advance Praise

"In a day when we are inundated with trivial information, it is delightfully refreshing to stumble upon a rich repository of practical wisdom. *Redeeming Work* is a surprisingly rare and priceless find for anyone who desires to pursue a life well lived. Integrating timeless wisdom as well as the latest social science research, Bryan Dik brings a welcome and much needed voice to the crucially important matter of discerning and living into one's calling. I highly recommend it!"

—TOM NELSON, DMin, president of Made to Flourish and author of *Work Matters: Connecting Sunday Worship to Monday Work*

"For years I've been waiting for this book to be written. In the Christian community we needed someone who could weave Biblical and theological frameworks with on-the-ground research about work and calling. Now Bryan Dik has cultivated this intersection. With great clarity, he describes social science findings about gift assessments, occupational connections, job search processes, and changing work dynamics. But, most importantly, this book provides a big frame through which to understand our Christian callings, as people created, challenged, redeemed, and contributing within God's story. Bryan's scholarship, examples, and commentary are powerful tools for guiding our lives and finding Christian joy in the process. I will recommend this book to my friends, fellow church members, professional colleagues, and adult children."

—SHIRLEY J. ROELS, PhD, executive director, International Network for Christian Higher Education

"Do you have eyes that see? One of the most ancient of questions, it is still one of the most important questions, running through the meaning of everyone's life and labor. In *Redeeming Work*, the seamless character of our work in the world is set forth with unusual clarity. Thinking across the disciplines, especially the richness of theological vision and the rigor of scientific insight, Bryan Dik brings years of thoughtful reflection on why work matters, and how we find our way into work that matters— yes, developing eyes to see why our work is integral to the very work of God. University students anywhere and everywhere, on their way into the rest of life, will be graced by a careful reading of this good book."

—**STEVEN GARBER**, PhD, professor of marketplace theology, Regent College, and author of *Visions of Vocation: Common Grace for the Common Good*

"*Redeeming Work* offers a fresh, research-informed, and practical roadmap to help Christians discern their callings in the workplace. Drawing on timeless wisdom from Scripture and modern insights from vocational psychology, Dik wisely reminds the reader to start their discernment journey by locating one's own particular story within God's larger story."

—**DAVID W. MILLER**, PhD, director of Princeton University's Faith & Work Initiative

"*Redeeming Work* is an evidence-based book full of practical, actionable advice to Christians seeking to flourish in their work and their faith. To live your calling is a choice: Bryan Dik explains the research and provides the tools to help make that choice a reality in your life...today."

—**CHRISTINE B. WHELAN**, PhD, clinical professor, School of Human Ecology, University of Wisconsin, and author of *The Big Picture: A Guide to Finding Your Purpose in Life*

"*Redeeming Work* gives actionable advice to Christians seeking to discern their calling. Dr. Dik exquisitely positions his expertise in vocational psychology in the broader context of God's story—creation, fall, redemption, and renewal—helping people see the bigger picture of God's purpose for their work. Readers will find proven tools to both sharpen their hearing of God's call and to steward their gifts for the common good and for His glory."

—BILL PEEL, DMin, executive director of the Center for Faith & Work at LeTourneau University

"As followers of Jesus, we've been given redemption, and one way we give thanks is to respond to this gift in our life and work. *Redeeming Work* merges sound theological reasoning, solid research from vocational psychology, and practical guidance from the frontline of the workplace to guide readers through a process of discovery. This process of self-discovery and reflection equips the reader with the insight needed for full participation in Christ's ongoing work of redemption. *Redeeming Work* is a trustworthy and essential guide for any person of faith on a journey to discover his or her place of flourishing in this world."

—MICHAEL K. LE ROY, PhD, president, Calvin University

"*Redeeming Work* happens when God's truth in the Bible meets God's truth in vocational psychology. If you want practical advice for discerning your call, this book is for you. Dr. Bryan Dik has spent much of his life pursuing the integration of faith and work. His deep faith and his expertise in vocational psychology bring new evidence-based wisdom to the vocational discernment process. Terrific book."

—JOHN VAN SLOTEN, author of *Every Job a Parable* and *The Day Metallica Came to Church*

"Bryan Dik offers an excellent resource for Christians who worry about whether their careers 'line up' with God's plan for their lives. The author takes his readers' theological commitments seriously, but coaxes them away from certain 'half-truths' that tend to become obstacles to discerning a call *('I should just pray and wait'* or *'I'm not good at this work, but God still wants me to do it')*. Dik's step-by-step suggestions make this book useful not only for young people who are discerning their future vocations, but for anyone interested in setting out in a new direction—as well as those who simply want to understand how their current career paths reflect their deeper callings."

—**DAVID S. CUNNINGHAM**, PhD, director, Network for Vocation in Undergraduate Education, Council of Independent Colleges, and professor of religion, Hope College

REDEEMING WORK

REDEEMING
WORK

A GUIDE TO DISCOVERING GOD'S CALLING FOR YOUR CAREER

BRYAN J. DIK, PhD

TEMPLETON
PRESS

Templeton Press
300 Conshohocken State Road, Suite 500
West Conshohocken, PA 19428
www.templetonpress.org

Set in Arnhem Blond by Gopa&Ted2, Inc.
Library of Congress Control Number: 2019955059

ISBN: 978-1-59947-539-4 (paperback)
ISBN: 978-1-59947-540-0 (ebook)

This paper meets the requirements of ANSI/NISO Z39.48-1992
(Permanence of Paper).
A catalogue record for this book is available from
the Library of Congress.

20 21 22 23 24   10 9 8 7 6 5 4 3 2 1
Printed in the United States of America.

To my parents,
Jack and Sandra Dik,
a constant source of encouragement
and models of living in
new creation hope.

Contents

Acknowledgments

W RITING A BOOK often feels like a solitary activity, but anyone who has done it will tell you it takes a village to pull off. That was certainly true for this book. Thanks are due first of all to the team at Templeton Press—Susan Arellano, Angelina Horst, Dan Reilly, and Trish Vergilio. They once again managed to combine vision, encouragement, patience, and expert editorial guidance in life-giving ways. I am also indebted to several friends and colleagues who offered extremely valuable, generative feedback on various drafts of the manuscript. Andy Tix especially was a workhorse in this regard. If he wasn't such an incredible teacher, he could easily find work as an editor, such are his gifts. Others who provided this assistance were Jack Dik, Terry Gray, Scott Filkin, Kaitlyn Reed, Amy Van Guilder Dik, and Paige Wiley. I am also indebted to the kingdom workers who allowed me the honor of sharing their stories in these pages.

I am blessed to work with a mighty team at jobZology. I am especially grateful to my cofounders Travis Hevelone, Kurt Kraiger, and Eric Leftwich, whose support of my vision for this project has meant the world. I am grateful to serve on the psychology faculty at Colorado State University as well, where I have the freedom to take on projects like this one. Thanks are due to my helpful colleagues there, as well as my PhD students who more than once had to wait longer than they should have for comments on their drafts because I needed to hit a deadline for this book. I am grateful as well for ongoing encouragement from my friends and frequent collaborators Ryan Duffy and Michael Steger, and to the broader community of calling and meaningful work researchers, faith and work scholars, and Society for Vocational Psychology colleagues, all of whom I value although will not name, lest I inadvertently miss anyone.

I owe a special debt of gratitude to Andrew and Heather Storteboom and Craig and Carolyn Hanson, who provided the sacred space needed for critical sessions of deep work. This book would never have come together, at least not in a timely way, without their kind hearts and generous spirits. I wish to thank my brothers and sisters in Christ at Immanuel Christian Reformed Church as well, especially our small group, who regularly checked in and offered support and prayer. Jo-Ida Hansen and Wayne Joosse continue to offer mentoring and friendship, and Craig Bierenga, Chris Kuipers, Matt Schaap, Matt Schlimm, and Zach Vandenberg are always on standby, which I have never taken for granted.

I am thankful to all the Van Guilders, to Luke LaBlance for checking on my progress, to the VandenBosch and Dukes families, and to my parents, Jack and Sandra, whose listening ears and constant encouragement have always given me a boost. Finally and most of all, thank you to my beautiful and brilliant wife, Amy, for her wisdom and sacrificial love, and to our fun-loving boys, Eli, Silas, Abram, and Jasper. My life is so much richer because you five are in it, and I thank God for you every day.

REDEEMING WORK

Introduction: Yearning for Integration

DOES GOD have a calling for me?
If so, how do I discern it?
What is God's will for my career path?
What are my gifts?
Where can I most effectively use them to serve in God's king dom—and how do I make that happen?

These are a few questions (among many) that matter deeply to Christians who want their faith to matter more than just on Sunday, but throughout all aspects of life, including their careers. These questions matter deeply to me. They were front and center for me early on, when as a college student, I tried very hard, but not very successfully, to gain a sense of direction for my career.

It's not that no career paths interested me. Quite the opposite—I was interested in lots of things, and the thought of choosing one path to the exclusion of other appealing paths was almost paralyzing. I clearly remember my daily retreats to one of several prayer rooms on campus, each outfitted with a kneeling bench, a Bible, and not much else. I spent long stretches of time with my knees on those benches, pleading with God to reveal his will for my life and my career, open to just about anything. I just wanted an answer. Desperately.

I don't think I expected an audible voice or a Moses-in-the-desert, burning bush–type sign. I did, however, expect that God would reveal his will to me with palpable certainty. I assumed that one day I would have an aha burst of insight, maybe during one of these prayer sessions. Or perhaps I would wake up one morning and simply *know*. When that inspired clarifying event didn't arrive, I prayed for it harder and waited longer. Unfortunately, the moment of spiritual awakening I sought never materialized, certainly not in the way I expected.

Eventually I did discern a calling. Ironically enough, I have since spent my entire career studying how people can discern and live their callings in life and work. How might people gain the kind of clarity and purpose I was seeking then? The answers are not always intuitive for Christians who have been socialized to adopt the pray-and-wait approach that defined my strategy at the time. But there are indeed answers. That's what this book is all about.

Redeeming Work offers practical answers to the tough questions that Christians ask about their career paths, questions like:

- How do I discern God's calling for me?
- How am I unique, and what difference does it make?
- How do I find a job that will enable me to live my calling?
- How does God's story impact what I do all day?

As Christians, we want to glorify God in our work. We want to feel confident that we are following God's will in our career decisions. But it is not easy. Today's work world is, in many ways, intimidating. Change is inevitable and constant, employer loyalty feels like a quaint relic of a bygone era, and robots are supposedly coming for all our jobs. The need for redemption in all areas of work is obvious. Forging a faith-driven career path is hard, and yet the need to do so has arguably never been greater.

Faith, Work, and Vocational Psychology

The need to more fully integrate faith and work is nothing new. Christians have navigated this topic for the full duration of Christian history—from Adam and Eve's earliest instruction in the Garden to the first Christians casting their fishing nets, from medieval monks scrubbing floors in drafty monasteries to business leaders meeting for prayer in a conference room somewhere near you. Christians haven't always agreed on how faith and work ought to relate, of course, but the question has ancient roots.

In more recent history, the desire for answers to faith and work questions has intensified. In fact, an identifiable faith and work movement has been building for decades, starting around the mid-1980s[1] and picking up steam as Millennials and now Gen Z pour into the workforce with aspirations for their work to reflect their deepest values. Many helpful resources have emerged from this movement, and key initiatives—networking groups, think tanks, conferences, and so on—are now in place among Christians of all stripes, driven by a spirit of cooperation to explore how God's story for the whole world ought to impact our work, no matter what that work entails. If you like books, many are available that explore this topic. In fact, a review of *hundreds* of books on faith and vocation was published *back in 2002*.[2] My shelves are full of such books, many of which I've found extremely helpful.

Yet as a believer in Christ and a vocational psychologist, one thing has always struck me as almost totally absent from the expanding collection of faith and work resources: science—more specifically, psychological science that has directly investigated career development, calling, and vocation. There are

decades of research within my field—vocational psychology—
that address key questions, including:

- Which factors influence well-being in people's careers?
- What career counseling activities lead to the best
  outcomes?
- How do people discern a sense of calling in their careers?
- What difference does it make when people approach
  their work as a calling?

Unfortunately, this research is almost universally overlooked in
the books that Christians read on faith and work.

I understand why this is the case. The vast majority of faith
and work resources have been written by pastors, theologians,
and business leaders—authors guided by Scripture, experience,
and wisdom from which I've benefited enormously. Yet these
same authors do not generally read and seldom even have access
to social science research. I've long been concerned about the
ivory-tower phenomenon in which scholars expend tremendous effort conducting rigorous research that is only ever read
by other scholars, and that fails to have any meaningful impact
on people's everyday lives. Reflecting on this problem, and
frustrated by the near-total absence of psychological research
in the faith and work conversation, I found myself thinking,
*Someone really should write a book that shares what we've learned
in vocational psychology with Christians interested in integrating
their faith with their work.* Then came, *Huh . . . maybe I should do
this.* And finally, *Who is going to do it, if I don't?* My sincere hope
is that *Redeeming Work* becomes a key resource to offer Christians evidence-based assistance to help them flourish in their
work, a resource informed by Scripture, theology, experience,
and cutting-edge psychological research.

Who Should Read This Book?

If questions related to discerning a calling and living out your faith at work strike a chord with you, or if you're simply curious about what a faith-informed career path might look like, this book is for you. Many of the concerns Christians have about discerning and living their callings become pressing for the first time during young adulthood. That's when, for many of us, the real world hits us in the face like a two-by-four, and we feel the pressure of making major life decisions in a way we had never before experienced. For this reason, many of this book's examples speak directly to young adults. Yet discerning and living a calling are not onetime events but rather represent an ongoing process. It is a lifelong journey, and at every stage, Christians want their faith intimately tied to what they do. *Redeeming Work* does not address retirement—a rich topic that deserves its own set of resources. But for adults of any age who are navigating career transitions and decision points, the biblical and scientifically informed advice in these pages is relevant now.

Where We Are Headed

The purpose of *Redeeming Work* is to give practical, actionable advice to Christians seeking to discern their callings and live out their faith within their careers. The book draws from wisdom derived from Scripture and vocational psychology, two of God's great gifts for people who want their faith to matter in their work. Part 1—"Foundations"—lays out the book's basic approach. The first chapter summarizes Scripture's Four-Act Story, noting how framing your personal story within the context of God's larger story offers the most promising pathway possible for experiencing joy, meaning, and purpose in your work.

The second chapter digs into several common, well-intentioned half-truths that Christians too often hold when they make decisions about their careers, often with disappointing results.

Part 2 walks through a process for "Discerning Your Calling." Chapter 3 suggests a strategy for staying spiritually grounded during a time of discernment, then explores what vocational psychologists know about what works in career decision-making. Results from that research translate into practical steps you can follow in your discernment process. Wise career decisions ordinarily start with an accurate understanding of one's gifts. In chapter 4, I invite you to take inventory of your interests, work values, and personality. As a reader, you can create a profile with PathwayU, an evidence-based online assessment system, and complete scientifically supported measures of these gifts. Access to PathwayU (powered by jobZology, a career assessment company I had the privilege of cofounding) is a unique feature of this book, and one of the ways it leverages psychological science to provide meaningful guidance. Once you identify the core features of your gifts, you can use this information in chapter 5 to evaluate the fit of diverse career paths. As you sift through your options, you will notice themes emerging in the paths that fit you well, and that align with your emerging sense of calling. Chapter 6 closes this part by describing an evidence-based approach to securing a job that aligns with your gifts and supports your goals for living your calling.

Finally, part 3—"Living Your Calling"—explores how to express a calling in today's economy. Chapter 7 tackles a key question of enormous relevance to Christians: "How can my faith help me succeed in the changing world of work?" Massive changes are under way in today's workplace, stemming from a new type of relationship between employers and workers, ubiquitous computing, and rapidly increasing automation. How is work transforming, and how should Christians navigate this? What is in many ways a challenge is also an opportunity for believers in Christ, a key point we explore in this chapter. Chapter 8 digs deeply into the Christian vision of redemption and renewal—which build on a high view of, and profound respect for, the goodness of creation. A major role assigned to humans in the Bible is that of partnering with Christ as "ministers of reconciliation" (2 Corinthians 5:18) throughout the whole creation, including every area of work. Christians who embrace this role often struggle with the details of what "working redemptively" means exactly, in the context of their jobs. This chapter explores this question, with an eye toward embracing how our work today contributes to God's work of making all things new.

Our careers are not the most important aspect of our lives, nor do they define our identity. That is found in Christ himself. Yet in his wisdom, God created people with common needs and the ability to meet them through mutual service. Whether we are employed, volunteer, or engage in caregiving (or all of these), most adults spend more of their waking hours working than doing anything else. Work is a core life role and a primary path through which we can express our gifts in the world, for God's glory. Perhaps you're reading this book because you are struggling to discern and live out your calling right now, maybe for the first time, or maybe after many seasons of discernment and re-engagement. Perhaps you're simply interested in learning more about what integrating faith and work might look like for Christians. Whatever the details of your personal story, you are part of God's larger story. That's where *Redeeming Work* begins.

PART 1

Foundations

CHAPTER 1

Fusing Faith and Life at Work

SOME TIME ago I attended a conference for Christian twenty- and thirty-somethings. The theme of the conference, held at a megachurch in a Denver suburb, was "Fusing Faith and Life." I had been looking forward to attending for weeks, especially the breakout session for professionals wanting to "fuse faith and life" in the workplace. I had a vested interest in the topic. As a then-new professor who had just started studying how people approach work as a calling or vocation, I was curious to learn what people might say about this topic—but my interest went much deeper than that. On a very personal level, I still had questions about how I could most effectively serve Christ's kingdom within the large, public research university where I worked. I relished the chance to hear from like-minded peers trying to live out their faith in their careers.[3]

The room that was allocated for the session was the church nursery, and the number who attended was, I can only assume, far more than the conference organizers had anticipated. With only a handful of adult-sized chairs, most of us were seated on the carpeted floor in a large circle around the room's perimeter. No lecture or workshop had been planned; this was intended to be a discussion. The session moderator opened by thanking everyone for coming and then asked, "What are some ways that each of you 'fuse faith and life' in your work?"

There was a very long pause. Finally, before the silence became too awkward, a woman cleared her throat and spoke.

"The main way that I do this," she said enthusiastically, "is to request time off to go on short-term mission trips with my church. My boss has been very supportive."

Heads nodded in approval. A second person raised his hand.

"I try really hard to get to know my coworkers well, because you never know when you might have an opportunity to share your faith with them."

More nodding heads; people could relate to this. A few other variations on these two themes—take time off for short-term mission trips and witness to your coworkers—emerged in the discussion that followed. Then people began sharing struggles. One woman, new to the insurance industry, voiced near-despair over how hard it was to work in her office as a Christian when so many of her fellow sales associates used deceptive tactics to take advantage of clients. Someone in the room advised her to share the love of Christ with her coworkers. If that doesn't do the trick, he advised, look for another job.

I was a bit dismayed by where this was heading. I raised my hand and said something along these lines: "Let's just take it as a given that we are called to support missions, and to be witnesses of Jesus's love wherever we find ourselves. For sure, these are critical responsibilities. Still, what about how we engage the work itself? If we truly believe Christ is Lord over every corner of creation, what does that mean for each of us, day to day, in our jobs?" I wanted to direct the conversation to the thorny issues I most wanted to discuss: Discerning our callings when we feel frozen with uncertainty. Exploring how our God-given gifts can help us address what is most needed in our professions. Promoting Christian ethics in environments often hostile to faith. Trying to understand how our approach to the daily grind can reflect our belief that Jesus is Lord not only of our spiritual lives but of *every* aspect of our lives—indeed, of the full expanse of his creation.

Instead, my question was met with uncomfortable silence.

If you are reading this book and you are a Christian, how would you answer the moderator's question: What are some examples of how you fuse faith and life in your career right now? If you're just starting out, how do you *hope* or *expect* to integrate your faith with your work as you look ahead? Your answer probably reflects what you believe about how the story of your career fits within the broader story of God's plan for the world. This is not a small matter. Your understanding of how the Bible impacts your work can mean the difference between spending your workdays counting down the minutes until quitting time or engaging your career with excitement, purpose, and a profound sense of meaning.[4] Yet many Christians have a hard time seeing how their work is relevant to their faith at all, much less supported by it. The chief reason for this? Too many Christians hold a view of God's story that is too narrow in scope.

Orient to God's Story (All of It)

When asked to explain the story of Scripture, many Christians start by sharing how people are separated from God because of their sin. Wholly unable to earn salvation by our own merit, we are in dire need of a savior. Having compassion on us, God sent his son, Jesus Christ, to earth. He lived a sinless life, taught us how to live, died a brutal death on the cross, and was resurrected three days later, before ascending into heaven. He lives today and offers new life to those who believe in him. By placing our trust in Jesus, we are saved from our sin and can look forward to living eternally in his presence.

Sin and salvation.

The problem is simple and powerful, laying out both the problem—our radical separation from God because of our sin—and the solution: Jesus entered the world to save us and reconnect us with God. All this is good and true, and the hope and peace it produces in people as they invest in a deepening relationship with Christ is beautiful.

Yet it is also incomplete. It represents an abridged vision of what the Bible teaches. It is amazingly good news, but it is not the whole story.

Since at least Augustine, theologians have approached Scripture as a unified narrative comprising several key sequential themes. In recent decades, Anglican bishop N. T. Wright popularized the idea that those themes unfold like acts of a play. In this book I refer to the whole of Scripture using this metaphor, as a play with four acts[5]—creation, fall, redemption, and renewal—a grand narrative that helps Christians understand how their own personal stories fit within God's larger story. For a more thorough discussion of the Bible's Four-Act Story, read the appendix, but here is a quick summary:[6]

- *Creation* describes the way things were, when God made a world[7] designed to flourish in unity, wholeness, and peace, where everything is the way it's supposed to be. The Bible calls that kind of flourishing *shalom*. God created humans in his own image and gave us the responsibility to care for and develop his creation, stewarding it and coaxing out its created potential (Genesis 1:28).
- The *fall* describes the way things are, broken and twisted because of sin. Adam and Eve's rebellion in Genesis 3 created a chasm between people and God. But it was

much broader than that; the entire creation was affected and is now "paradise lost"—a distorted version of what God intended for it.

- *Redemption* describes how God reclaimed all things through the life, death, and resurrection of Jesus Christ. Redemption "has accomplished nothing less than the promise of a restored paradise," writes Amy Sherman, "where shalom in all its dimensions will reign."[8] That restored paradise is the new heavens and the new earth, initiated with the first fruits of Christ's resurrection and the fullness of the Holy Spirit. Right now, you and I are the instruments of God's redemptive work, his agents of renewal, partners with Christ in making all things new.

- *Renewal* describes the way things will be, when Christ returns and heaven comes to earth. "He will wipe every tear from their eyes," taught John the Apostle. "There will be no more death or mourning or crying or pain, for the old order of things has passed away" (Revelation 21:4). The "old order" refers to sin and its effects on creation, which will be finally renewed as God intended: "He who was seated on the throne said, 'I am making everything new!'" (Revelation 21:5).

The sin-and-salvation view that permeated the breakout session at that Fusing Faith and Life conference fails to capture all four acts of this story. It is only a Two-Act Story, one that focuses on the fall and a narrow vision of redemption (specifically, our restored relationship with God) without placing our sin and Christ's work on the cross in their broader context. Those two acts are absolutely critical, but the full context is essential for three reasons:

- *The Two-Act Story doesn't tell us our purpose.* With its focus on the fall, the Two-Act Story emphasizes human shortcomings without affirming that, despite our sin, we are made in God's image and given work to do. The Four-Act Story recognizes that, from the very beginning, God gave people a grand mission: caring for and cultivating his creation, for his glory.

- *The Two-Act Story forces a sacred-secular separation.* The Two-Act Story draws a hard line between sacred and secular spheres of life; mission work and evangelism are sacred, and everything else is secular. The Four-Act Story, in contrast, recognizes that Christ is Lord of every square inch of creation; *all* of it is sacred. God cares about everything we do and is glorified within any honest area of work, not just "church work."

- *The Two-Act Story equates redemption with escape.* Emphasizing redemption without focusing on renewal implies that our personal salvation and entrance into heaven are God's endgame. If that were the case, none of our work (other than spreading the gospel) would matter—but this isn't what the Bible teaches. Our salvation is a sacred gift, to be sure. Yet that gift comes with responsibilities that include, but go far beyond, evangelism. The Four-Act Story emphasizes that we are not only saved but saved for a purpose—that of bringing God glory and partnering with Christ to make all things new, anticipating the new heavens and the new earth (Revelation 21). *That* is God's endgame.

In short, the Two-Act Story is only part of the whole story. Because of what it leaves out, the Two-Act Story offers precious little to inform the integration of faith with the rest of life in general, and with work in particular. The two strategies that emerged in the discussion at that conference—going on mission trips[9] and sharing our faith with coworkers[10]—are clearly both *good things*. But as strategies for fusing faith and life at work, they fall woefully short. Neither has anything to do with the day-to-day details of work itself. Taking time off to go on mission trips is actually the *opposite* of integrating faith and work; it amounts to leaving our work to live out our faith elsewhere. And while we are absolutely called in Scripture to look for Spirit-led opportunities to share our faith wherever we are, evangelism doesn't have much to do with the specifics of plumbing or manufacturing or nursing or science or software. On their own, these are strategies for *separating*, not fusing, faith and life within our work. If the Two-Act Story forms the lens through which you view your job, you will struggle to see any eternal significance in your work, unless you work in a formal ministry role.

In contrast, the Four-Act Story offers a vision for how the truth of Scripture transforms not only our personal lives but all areas of life, including every area of work. It functions like a pair of glasses that helps us focus on God's grand plan and orient our lives to that plan. Left to ourselves, our vision is blurry; we do our best, but there is so much we fail to see. Through these glasses, things come into focus. God created everything good, but sin distorted that creation. Yet God redeemed it in Jesus Christ and is making all things new. Right now, God calls us to serve as his agents of renewal. It is an awesome privilege, one that infuses any honest type of work with soul-stirring purpose.[11]

What does this look like, practically? Consider Jen, a baker and entrepreneur who orients to the Four-Act Story in how she runs the Sweet Petite, a bakery specializing in gluten-free cakes that double as gorgeous works of art.[12] Jen is an art school graduate and views her desserts as opportunities to create. "I think aesthetic beauty is really important," she notes. "God gave beauty. He gave amazing art and amazing things to create with—and cake is basically just edible sculpture. And people love it—and people with an aversion to wheat, they are really excited that there is something out there that they can have for a birthday or a holiday or whatever." Jen's cakes bring forth God's good creation—they are truly beautiful. Yet there is more than beauty in Jen's work; there is justice and grace. All too often, people with severe dietary intolerances begin to view "good food" as simply off-limits, a dietary manifestation of fallen creation groaning.[13] The Sweet Petite offers redemptive grace by making beautiful, delicious cakes available to everyone, including those with dairy and wheat sensitivities, sending the symbolic message that God's kingdom feast is available to all who wish to partake.

As is the case for Jen, the joy we experience as we draw from the biblical narrative—God's story and our place within it—to support and sustain our work is incredibly life-giving. The Creator and Sustainer of the universe has granted all of us the mandate to cultivate creation and to partner in restoring to wholeness those places where things have gone awry. What could possibly make work more meaningful than that?

Scripture, Science, and Career Decision-Making

Understanding the Bible's full scope is necessary to appreciate God's larger story. Yet the Bible is not an encyclopedia or instruction manual that directly addresses every problem of living in the modern world.[14] For example, the Bible teaches Christians to work at whatever they do with all their hearts "as working for the Lord" (Colossians 3:23), but it does not describe how to change a car's timing belt, cultivate a soybean field so that it produces a high yield, or prepare a soufflé that doesn't collapse. The Bible also teaches Christians to be good stewards of the resources with which they've been entrusted (Matthew 25:14–30), but it does not steer them toward the most effective retirement investment strategy or the optimum smartphone plan for their usage. Building on the Bible's foundation, we turn to other sources of information to address those questions wisely. Similarly, Christians on the job market know how to approach the search process with integrity, but they also know they must look elsewhere for practical guidance on how to formal a résumé or prep for a job interview. Even answers to the question "How should I discern God's calling for my career?" are not directly provided in Scripture.[15]

When it comes to making decisions about their career paths, Christians are wise to use a prayerful discernment process that follows the Bible's directives for seeking God's will for their lives. As we'll see shortly, the Bible reveals much about God's will, but the question of God's specific plan for what you ought to do next is a complicated matter. Wisdom is required when making such decisions. I discuss this in much greater detail later, but discernment questions not directly addressed in Scripture ought to be informed by what research shows actually helps people who face these kinds of decisions. These questions are critical: What *does* help, and how do we know? What kinds of activities, exercises, interactions, and considerations lead people with career concerns toward good outcomes? Vocational psychologists have systematically investigated these questions and others like them. This book presents answers that have emerged to date that can help Christians discern their callings and that apply directly to your own discernment process.

The Difference a Calling Makes

While I was working as a counselor in my PhD program's career assessment clinic, I repeatedly heard clients yearn for meaning in their work. Some used the word "calling" to describe what they were after: a career that synced with their broader sense of purpose in life. I had already been reading broadly from books on calling and vocation, faith and work—nearly all of them in the practical theology genre. Naturally, I was also curious about psychologists' take on the matter, so I conducted an extensive search to locate every empirical study of calling and vocation that had ever been published in the social sciences.[16] At that time, as I recall, I found a grand total of eight such studies *in all of history.*

Many of these studies conceptualized "calling" in what felt to me like a watered-down, humanistic version of what was described so richly in all those books on faith and work. Is a calling just another word for a passion? Does discerning a calling really mean turning inward to find the path that will bring me the most happiness? I didn't think so then, and I don't think so now. A calling recognizes a caller—the issuer of the call. And a calling recognizes that our work is not for ourselves, first and foremost. Instead, a calling is a pathway through which we can express our gifts for the common good, and for God's glory. The need for more psychological research on work as a calling was obvious to me, especially research that aligned with a distinctly Christian understanding of the concept. Aware that I had the training to carry out this kind of research, I started to see it as a way I could use my gifts to contribute something of value. For me, this was a moment when I felt a real sense of clarity for what God was calling me to do with my life.

Some time has passed since I had that realization, enough time to land a faculty job at a world-class university, develop a network of gifted collaborators, and establish a program of research on calling. To inform that research, I defined a *calling* as a transcendent summons toward purposeful work motivated by a desire to make a positive difference.[17] Next, I led a team that designed a set of scales to measure people's perception of a calling[18] and began using those scales to investigate the difference it makes when people approach their work that way. The number of empirical studies on calling has since grown exponentially,[19] and we've learned an enormous amount from them. For example:

- *A sense of calling is surprisingly prevalent.* Among students and employed adults, anywhere from one-third to two-thirds indicate that the concept of calling is relevant to how they view their work. One study using a national sample discovered that 42 percent of U.S. adults responded "mostly true" or "totally true" to the item "I have a calling to a particular line of work."[20]
- *A sense of calling is linked with positive career development outcomes.* People who feel they have a calling, compared to other people who do not, are more confident they can make good decisions about their careers, more committed to their jobs and organizations, more motivated and engaged, and more satisfied with their jobs.
- *A sense of calling is associated with general well-being.* Compared to those without a sense of calling, those with callings are happier, more satisfied with life, cope more effectively with challenges, and express a stronger sense of meaning and purpose in their lives.

- *It's not only about having it; it's about living it.* People who
  believe they have a calling are happiest, most committed, and experience the most benefit when they are working in a role that enables them to live out their calling.
  Sadly, some people have trouble finding opportunities
  that permit them to do this. As a result, they may feel
  frustrated, discouraged, unhappy, and even depressed.
- *A sense of calling can have some drawbacks, too.* People
  willingly make tough sacrifices to pursue their callings
  and sometimes trade some types of satisfaction and
  well-being for others (e.g., material wealth and comfort
  for a sense of contribution). Pursuing a calling can also
  sometimes make people vulnerable to problems like
  workaholism, burnout, poor work-family balance, and
  exploitation by unscrupulous employers.

The rest of this book walks you through how you can discern and live God's calling within your career path, leaning on
points of convergence in the foundation of Scripture and the
findings of psychological science. As you embark on this journey, think back on God's Four-Act Story. Each act—creation, fall,
redemption, renewal—raises key questions to address as you
move forward in your career. What is God's creational design for
the areas of responsibility that define the career paths you are
considering? How do (or how will) the effects of the fall influence your experiences at work? What possibilities do you see for
redemption and renewal? I repeat these questions throughout
this book. Each of us has a path to navigate, our own niche for
which these questions matter. But some other questions are also
relevant: How can you discern your calling as it applies to your
career? What is God's will for you? What if you don't feel well-
equipped? In response to questions like these, well-meaning

Christians often lean on assumptions that are not completely true. Questions like these, and the half-true advice that often is dispensed in response to them, are matters we tackle in the next chapter.

CHAPTER 2

"God Doesn't Call the Equipped, He Equips the Called" and Other Half-Truths

FAITH-WORK INTEGRATION is a goal for many Christians, but the Christian community often makes integration a lot harder than it needs to be. I was reminded of this while working with Nate. When I first met him, Nate was a twenty-one-year-old honors student in search of a thesis adviser. He wanted to develop a project that focused on his Christian worldview, and a colleague suggested he contact me for assistance. Nate showed up to our first meeting wearing a Detroit Tigers hat—the classic navy-blue home lid with the white old English "D." After a firm handshake, I pointed to the hat and asked, "Are you a fan?" In the conversation that followed, a few things became clear. The first was that Nate was a sports aficionado who possessed as deep a knowledge base of pro teams in Detroit as anyone I had ever encountered. (As a Michigan native and fairly obsessive sports fan myself, I found this very endearing.) He wasn't only a fan, either—he worked part-time in the sports communications division of Colorado State's athletic department. He attended multiple Rams home games per week and often traveled with teams when they competed on the road, tweeting highlights of game action and pulling together press releases to promote the team. He loved it and was strongly considering opportunities in that field after he graduated.

The second thing that quickly became obvious was Nate's sincere Christian faith. His relationship with Jesus was clearly the most important thing in his life, and he was heavily involved in our university's chapter of the Navigators, the campus ministry group. He also shared that he had received a lot of feedback suggesting he pursue a career as a pastor, a possibility that weighed heavily on his mind. Some of this feedback was undoubtedly rooted in the fact that Nate was a charmer, extraverted and winningly authentic, every bit a leader. He also communicated well, both in public speaking (for which he had no fear) and as a blogger.[21] When a student like Nate emerges as a mature believer in Christ with leadership skills, the gift of gab, and a knack for sharing about Scripture in front of a room, it doesn't take long for fellow Christians to urge him to consider formal ministry.

I encouraged Nate to tackle a thesis topic that occupied the points where some of the central passions in his life converged. He loved this plan. Over the next several months, he crafted a fifty-page essay exploring the implications of the Bible's Four-Act Story on sports, communications, and the intersection of the two. Nate wrote about God's apparent creational design for sports communication, the ways it seems distorted by sin, and opportunities for redemption, culminating in "practical guidelines for any person seeking to live biblically while employed in an Athletics Communications position."[22] It was a rigorous, well-reasoned, thoroughly excellent piece of work.

On the day he presented the project to his thesis committee, Nate got personal. He shared how he had wrestled with the question of whether, as a Christian, it made sense to devote so much of his time and energy to sports. It was a passion, but wouldn't it be better to focus on ministry? Two years prior, this inner battle had escalated, and Nate resolved it by quitting his athletic department internship. But the decision didn't stick; he soon returned. He could not escape his captivation with sports, and ultimately determined that the Christian faith and sports were emphatically *not* mutually exclusive. Sports could be an idol if viewed as an ultimate thing rather than a good thing, or if people put sports (or a team or athlete) in front of their devotion to God. But when viewed in their proper place, aren't sports part of the wide array of good gifts God gives people to enjoy, for his glory? If that's the case, sports should be redeemed rather than avoided. In fact, Nate came to see this kind of Christian engagement in sports as an urgent need and developed a framework to guide that effort, with very practical directives.

Given that homerun of a learning outcome, I was not expecting what Nate said next.

"I've learned so much from this project," he said, "but I've decided I'm going to attend seminary next year and begin my training for the ministry."

His choice to pursue a traditional ministry role felt like a mismatch with the passion he expressed about the need for Christians to work redemptively in sports. After all that research and introspection, how did he arrive at this as his path forward? All the same, I congratulated Nate on his decision and offered to write a recommendation letter, should he need it.

About three months later, Nate called.

"If you're still willing, I could use that letter," he said. "Not for seminary though. I've decided to pursue a graduate degree in communications, and to work in an athletic department. I'm already admitted, I just need the letter as a formality."

"Wow," I said. "Congratulations! But tell me—what changed?"

Nate shared how he came to realize his sense of calling to the ministry was rooted in the feedback he received from people, always telling him he should become a pastor. All that encouragement felt good, but Nate asked himself, *Am I doing this for the right reasons? Am I doing this for God's glory or for mine?* He also noticed his motivation to stay engaged in sports was as strong as ever. Even if no one ever praised him for his work in the athletic department, he knew he'd love it. But how would he feel about a ministry career if all that positive reinforcement from people went away? He wasn't sure. In fact, he admitted he felt pressure to enter the ministry. He felt he would let people down if he pursued any other path. And part of him, he realized, believed if he was truly a good Christian, he'd *have* to become a pastor.

Things changed after an interaction with some track athletes who had met with Nate a couple times for prayer. One morning, while they prayed before a conference championship meet, one of the athletes expressed gratitude to God for Nate—not about his knack for public speaking, his leadership ability, or his potential in ministry, but simply for being there with them. "That was a lightbulb moment for me," Nate said. "That prayer made me realize that God was using me simply because I was trying to live out my faith in the place where I was, a place where Christians are needed, and that was enough." He prayed further, reflected on his experience, tested his motives, and talked it over with key mentors in his life. All these steps affirmed that sports communications is Nate's calling.

As I write this, Nate is wrapping up his final semester in that master's program and has loved every minute of it. "I've never looked back," he told me recently. "This doesn't feel like work. I have no regrets and I absolutely feel like I am doing the right thing. Now I realize, and embrace, that I can glorify God in this field. I feel like God is pleased with what I'm doing, and I'm no longer trying to force something that would have made other Christians happy but deep inside wasn't really what I wanted to do, or what God wanted me to do. God placed this inside of me. I just had to pay attention to it."

Despite his deep focus on Christ's lordship over all areas of life, and even recognizing both the profound need for Christians in sports and his own gifts in sports communication, Nate still felt pressure to pursue a traditional ministry career. He had internalized one of several half-truths—that "good Christians" need to consider ministry or missions before anything else—that we examine next. (Did you read Nate's story and feel disappointed that he changed course, leaving formal ministry before he even started, to pursue sports communications instead? If so, you may well share that internalized belief.) These half-truths may have honorable roots, but they miss what the Bible teaches. They sound reasonable, but they ultimately prove unhelpful, and sometimes harmful. Let's look carefully at four of these half-truths and evaluate them in light of biblical teaching and what psychological science reveals about God's created design for people as they discern and live out their callings.

HALF-TRUTH #1:
"If I'm serious about my faith, I should consider ministry and missions before anything else."

This statement is built on the Two-Act Story assumption that there is a hierarchy of callings: some are sacred, whereas others, while permissible, hold less spiritual significance. This has proven a hard viewpoint for Christians to shake.[23] Gordon T. Smith, president of Ambrose University, reflects on this:

> As a young man I remember those occasions when it was suggested that if we really loved the Lord we would be missionaries, and if not missionaries, then pastors, and if not missionaries or pastors, then at least business people (in "secular work") who could

support those with "sacred" callings. Within my tra-
dition this was captured in the words of A. B. Simpson, which would no doubt be typical of what many
would have heard as young people and perhaps still
hear today: "Your only excuse for staying home and
not going to the mission field is if by staying home you
can do more to further the cause of missions than by
going." While the motive behind such a statement is
noble, I dare think what it has meant for so many who
because of such a perspective have failed to affirm and
celebrate the sacredness of their work. Though we
have made major progress, this narrow understanding of vocation does not die easily.[24]

The message might be subtler today, but it is still here. Nate's
experience illustrates this. So did the Fusing Faith and Life conference I described in the last chapter. There was an exhibit hall
at that conference, wall to wall with vendor booths. Nearly every
last one of them represented a missions organization. The message was not spelled out as explicitly as it was in A. B. Simpson's
quote, but it was impossible to ignore: if you really care about
fusing your faith with your life, you should become a missionary, or at least go on mission trips whenever you can.

That this is a half-truth means it is not a total falsehood; to
reiterate, ministry and missions are very important. We need
more good ministers and missionaries. But this half-truth is
problematic for at least two reasons.

First, it implies that anyone working outside of formal ministry or missions is not serious about their faith, at least not compared to pastors and missionaries. Experience tells us that this
is simply not true. Obviously, as a group, pastors and missionaries take their faith very seriously. Yet faith heroes and spiritual

role models can be found within any profession. More to the point, as we reviewed in the last chapter, Christ's lordship over his entire creation demands that Christians serve him everywhere; all of it is sacred, every corner. And while being serious about one's faith seems a necessary condition to serve as a pastor or missionary, it is far from sufficient. Anyone considering a career in ministry or missions should ask, *Do I have the gifts required to serve effectively in these roles?*

That brings us to the second reason this half-truth gets it wrong: it ignores the role of gifts in discerning a calling. Paul discusses gifts in several places in the New Testament. A good example is 1 Corinthians 12:4–7: "There are different kinds of gifts, but the same Spirit distributes them. There are different kinds of service, but the same Lord. There are different kinds of working, but in all of them and in everyone it is the same God at work. Now to each one the manifestation of the Spirit is given for the common good." The basic principle is straightforward: God grants us different gifts, and there are different roles in which those gifts can be expressed. Our responsibility is to work alongside others, each sharing our unique gifts collaboratively, in ways that advance the common good.[25]

As a Christian and a vocational psychologist, this is where I get excited, because what we've learned from research fits hand in glove with what Scripture teaches about gifts and callings. Psychologists have long studied "gifts," or characteristics that describe how people differ from each other in the world of work. In his classic book *Choosing a Vocation*, Frank Parsons, the "father of vocational guidance," laid out this deceptively simple three-part decision-making strategy:

In the wise choice of a vocation, there are three broad factors: (1) a clear understanding of yourself, your aptitudes, abilities, interests, ambitions, limitations, and their causes; (2) a knowledge of the requirements, conditions of success, advantages and disadvantages, compensation, opportunities, and prospects in different lines of work; and (3) true reasoning on the relations of these two groups of facts.[26]

The "true reasoning" is where the rubber hits the road; we dig into that step of Parson's model in chapters 3 and 4. The point is that this "person-environment fit" principle is exactly what Paul described when writing about gifts in the church.

This "diversity and unity in gifts" or person-environment fit notion has been tested in research too. Industrial-organizational psychologist Amy Kristof-Brown led a team that gathered every published study that had ever examined some aspect of person-environment fit—172 in all—to answer the question: does working in a role that fits a person's gifts predict positive outcomes? Sure enough, the researchers found that the greater the fit, the better the outcome—a pattern that held across multiple levels of fit (e.g., fit to occupation, fit to job, fit to organization, fit to one's work team, fit to a supervisor).[27] In short, fit really does matter.

Ministry and missions are vital, and central to the work of the church. Yet Scripture and psychological science converge on the importance of appealing to our gifts as a driver of vocational discernment. If your gifts make you well-suited to serve in a pastoral or missions role, perhaps God is calling you to pursue these paths. Otherwise, take a step back and prayerfully consider where your unique gifts have best equipped you to serve Christ's kingdom.

HALF-TRUTH #2:
"To discern my calling, I should pray and wait for God's direction."

Christians sometimes approach the task of discerning a calling by praying wholeheartedly for a divine revelation and expecting to receive one quickly and directly. If an answer does not follow, a common response is to pray harder and wait longer. This is the pray-and-wait approach to discernment, the strategy I used back in those college prayer rooms.

Like all the half-truths in this chapter, this approach gets it partly right. Christians should definitely pray over matters like this. Prayer from believers is "powerful and effective" (James 5:6). Christians are called to cast all their cares on God (1 Peter 5:7) and to pray all the time (1 Thessalonians 5:17). And research consistently finds that praying is good for us.[28] The problem is not with the prayer. It is with the waiting—or rather, with the passive approach to waiting I exhibited when I prayed for a divine revelation. Patience is a virtue, but such passive waiting amounts to a discernment strategy in which all the key clues are ignored. Imagine a detective investigating a crime by asking God to directly reveal who had committed it, without looking at the evidence. We'd probably consider that detective incompetent, irresponsible, or both. Obviously, God could reveal the perpetrator directly, if it pleased him to do so. But all the detective's forensic and investigative training, plus the legal requirements of building a case, demands that someone get to work. A Christian detective should pray, but pray for what? For insight, a clear mind, guidance in uncovering the right information, and wisdom in sorting through it. Even while still in prayer, a good detective would gather key data from myriad sources, put the evidence together, and follow where it leads.

Making career choices is like detective work. It requires gathering good information (e.g., about one's gifts and about various career paths), envisioning different possibilities, and consulting with trusted advisers to identify possible blind spots. It involves looking for consistencies that converge across multiple data sources. It takes patience and persistence, effort and wisdom. Dramatic calling experiences that reveal a clear answer sometimes happen, but they are rare. Theologians recognize this. "Though there are exceptions," writes Douglas Schuurman, "generally God uses mediators to call individuals to particular places of service."[29] By "mediators," Schuurman refers to your gifts, the world's needs, your other obligations in life, discussions with trusted mentors, and prayer. God grants you the ability to self-reflect, to examine your gifts, and to use available resources to help evaluate how your gifts fit with the world's needs and available opportunities. All these can help you discern your calling.

We explore discernment further in the next two chapters, but for now, rest assured: when Christians engage in active discernment guided by wisdom, the answers they are praying for usually emerge.

Half-Truth #3:
"If I'm not careful, I might miss my calling."

Some Christians desire a clear answer to the calling question because they worry they might choose the wrong career and become trapped in a chronically dissatisfying situation. This is similar to the concept of the soul mate in romantic relationships. The soul-mate notion, perpetuated by countless romantic comedies, can be summarized as "There is one person out there for me in the universe. (Probably another student at my university / guy who rides my same subway line / woman who uses my same Laundromat / etc.) If I don't find that person, I'll be doomed to a life of loneliness and misery." The career version is similar: "If I make the wrong choice and miss my calling, I'll end up struggling in a career outside of God's will."

Is it possible to approach your career decision-making in good faith, practice careful discernment, and end up completely missing the boat? Some Christians are afraid of ending up like Nancy Hollander, eulogized in this excerpt from the satirical news source *The Onion*:

97-Year-Old Dies Unaware of Being Violin Prodigy

ROCKFORD, IL—Retired post office branch manager Nancy Hollander, 97, died at her home of natural causes Tuesday, after spending her life completely unaware that she was one of the most talented musicians of the past century and possessed the untapped ability to become a world-class violin virtuoso.

She is survived by two daughters, a son, six grandchildren, and three great-grandchildren, all of whom will forever remain oblivious to the national treasure Hollander would have become had she just picked up a violin even once.

"We're really going to miss Mom—she was such a gentle, sensitive, perceptive person," said Hollander's son, David, unknowingly outlining qualities that would have infused his mother's interpretation of Mendelssohn's Violin Concerto with a singular, haunting beauty capable of moving the most jaded of souls. "Even though she never drew attention to herself, mom had such a strong, commanding presence."[30]

Is this how it works? Is it possible there is some latent ability buried so deep within that you risk limping through life without knowing it is there, going to your grave without ever realizing the incredible accomplishments you could have achieved had you only been privy to that talent? A related question: is there a single, specific path that God expects you to pursue, requiring that you identify it in detail before you ever set out to do anything?

The answer to all of these questions is no. Let's explore why.

God's will of decree and will of desire are clear in Scripture, but God's will of direction is another matter. All of us want to understand God's will for our lives, but what exactly does that mean? The Bible is clear about a couple of things we refer to as God's will.[31] One truth is that everything that happens, happens because of God's *will of decree*. Ephesians 1:11 notes that God "works out *everything* in conformity with the purpose of his will" (emphasis added). Jesus made the point this way: "Are not two sparrows sold for a penny? And not one of them will fall to the ground outside your Father's care. And even the very hairs of your head are all numbered" (Matthew 10:29–30). Everything, good and bad,[32] the big-picture themes and the minutia, all of it happens according to God's plan and purpose (Isaiah 46:9–10).

The second thing about which the Bible is clear is what God wants from us—his *will of desire*. Deuteronomy 29:29 hints at the difference between God's will of decree and will of desire: "The secret things belong to the LORD our God, but the things revealed belong to us and to our children forever, that we may follow all the words of this law." God's sovereign purpose is known only to God, but he has revealed certain things for us to understand and obey. There are many examples in Scripture. In Ephesians 5, doing God's will means, among other things, to "follow God's example," to "walk in the way of love," to expose "fruitless deeds of darkness," to "be filled with the Spirit," and to "sing and make music from your heart to the Lord, always giving thanks to God the Father for everything, in the name of our Lord Jesus Christ." In 1 John 2, doing God's will means avoiding fleshly desires and pride in our possessions (vv. 15–17). In 1 Thessalonians 5, doing God's will means to "rejoice always, pray continually," and "give thanks in all circumstances" (v. 18). I could keep going, but you get the point: God's will of desire means he wants us to walk with him in obedience.

It is God's *will of direction*, though, that Christians think of when grappling with what career to pursue. We know God has a plan for our lives, but why doesn't he make that plan easier to figure out? Anxiety over our ability to understand God's will of direction prompts Christians to fear making the wrong choice and living with the consequences of being "out of the center of his will." Pastor and author Kevin DeYoung addresses this concern head-on:

So here is the real heart of the matter: Does God have a secret will of direction that He expects us to figure out before we do anything? And the answer is no. Yes, God has a specific plan for our lives. And yes, we can be assured that He works things for our good in Christ Jesus. And yes, looking back we will often be able to trace God's hand in bringing us to where we are. But while we are free to ask God for wisdom, He does not burden us with the task of divining His will of direction for our lives ahead of time. The second half of that last sentence is crucial. God does have a specific plan for our lives, but it is not one that he expects us to figure out before we make a decision. I'm not saying God won't help you make decisions (it's called wisdom . . .). I'm not saying God doesn't care about your future. I'm not saying God isn't directing your path and in control amidst the chaos of your life. I believe in providence with all my heart. What I am saying is that we should stop thinking of God's will like a corn maze, or a tightrope, or a bull's-eye, or a choose-your-own-adventure novel.[33]

The fact that God seldom reveals a direct answer to our questions about what to do at each crossroads in our lives suggests that he grants us the freedom to make our own choices. That doesn't mean God is indifferent, or that any choice is a good choice. Throwing a dart at the classified ads or a college catalog is still a bad way to choose a career. But since we know God has a plan for our lives, our approach should be to make choices with wisdom. I will soon explore what this looks like, but the broader point is this: When you prayerfully approach the decision-making task with wisdom, you can go forward with confidence that God will fit your choices into his sovereign will.

For most of us, there is more than one right answer. Research suggests that people's unique profiles of work-related attributes (like interests, values, and personality)—their gifts—seem to prepare them well for success and satisfaction within particular clusters of occupations, rather than only within a narrow job title. If you have gifts for caregiving, putting together words in creative ways, training and teaching, or constructing and fixing mechanical systems, for example, each of these points to not one but several possible career paths. You could potentially pursue any of them while still being faithful to your calling, provided that you are using your gifts to glorify God and make the world better. Instead of feeling paralyzed by the fear of getting it wrong, you can feel energized by the freedom that comes from having multiple ways to get it right.

Discerning and living a calling represent an ongoing process, not a once-and-for-all event. A final point related to this half-truth is that if you can expect anything from making career choices, it is that whatever you choose will change. The average adult in the United States holds nearly a dozen jobs between ages eighteen and fifty.[34] One might see that statistic and assume that people cannot seem to get it right, so they keep changing jobs until they do. But this is not usually the case. Many people who have had long, satisfying careers will tell you their callings have evolved—that what was an excellent fit at one point in time led to new opportunities that became an even better fit at another point in time, which in turn fostered new skills that eventually led to other new pathways. In my research lab, we constructed subscales of our Calling and Vocation Questionnaire to measure the extent to which people perceived a calling or were searching for a calling. We expected scores on these subscales to correlate negatively, assuming people only search for a calling when they don't have one. Imagine our surprise, then, when scores were not only *positively* correlated, but so highly positively correlated we had to conclude that both scales were tapping into the same phenomenon. Ultimately, we concluded that this strong positive correlation conveyed that a calling is an ongoing process rather than a thing to be discovered. Almost by definition, part of having a calling means constantly asking questions like *How can I enhance or expand my sphere of influence? How can I use my gifts to serve the kingdom with greater impact? Are there other opportunities that would permit me to live my calling more effectively?* I ask myself these questions all the time. Living a calling is an entire lifestyle of serving faithfully while also listening to the Spirit's promptings, often communicated through new skills and new opportunities for service.

For all of these reasons, if you approach the task with wisdom, you do not have to fear making the wrong choice and missing your calling.

HALF-TRUTH #4:
"God doesn't call the equipped, he equips the called."

I recently attended a presentation by the leader of a large Christian organization who began by sharing how he ended up in his job. With genuine humility, he noted that he had never served in a role like this one. He had worked as a pastor and teacher, but never even entertained the thought of a CEO-type position until the organization's board called him up and requested a meeting. "We think that you are the ideal person to lead us," they told him. "Please, prayerfully consider it." He shared that as he did this, he felt a desire to take on the challenge, but that his desire was mixed with a strong sense of inadequacy, given how different his prior experiences were from what was in the job description. Could he really do this? He wasn't so sure. Then he told us he began feeling greater confidence when he remembered, "God doesn't call the equipped, he equips the called."

I suspect we all feel intimidated at times by a daunting set of work-related responsibilities. Christians are good at offering encouragement in this scenario with that well-trodden line: "God doesn't call the equipped, he equips the called." Some Christians say this with the same confidence they have when quoting Scripture. (I wonder, in fact, if some believe they *are* quoting Scripture, but you won't find this sentence in the Bible.) Let's be clear: God does equip the called. God's strength shines in people who own up to their weaknesses. Paul uses himself as an example in 2 Corinthians: "But he said to me, 'My grace is sufficient for you, for my power is made perfect in weakness.' Therefore, I will boast all the more gladly about my weaknesses, so that Christ's power may rest on me" (12:9). When we recognize our shortcomings, we depend less on our own talent and more on God's desire to work through us.

Still, to say that "God doesn't call the equipped" overlooks overwhelming biblical evidence to the contrary. Consider Moses. He is often cited as an example of how "God doesn't call the equipped" due to his lack of confidence in his public speaking ability. "But Moses pleaded with the LORD, 'Oh Lord, I'm just not a good speaker. I never have been, and I'm not now, even after you have spoken to me. I'm clumsy with words'" (Exodus 4:10 NLT). God responded by promising him help, before also offering Aaron, Moses's brother, as spokesman to the Hebrew people. Yet despite Moses's concerns about his ability as an orator, his upbringing gave him insights into Pharaoh's household that literally no other Hebrew possessed. After all, when still a baby, Moses floated in a basket to Pharaoh's daughter, who rescued and adopted him as her own son (Exodus 2:10). Who better to seek the release of Israelite slaves from Pharaoh than someone who was raised in Pharaoh's palace? God equips the called, and he also calls the equipped.

Christians also say "God doesn't call the equipped" and think of David, the little shepherd boy God summoned to kill Goliath, the Philistine giant-warrior who sent fear down the spines of the Israelite army. David was a little boy, wasn't he? Just about every children's Bible storybook in my house depicts him that way, as a wide-eyed, baby-faced eight-year-old. There is even a children's song: "Only a boy named David, only a little sling . . ." But while David was not an experienced soldier, he pointed out to Saul:

When a lion or bear came and carried off a sheep from the flock, I went after it, struck it and rescued the sheep from its mouth. When it turned on me, I seized it by its hair, struck it, and killed it. Your servant has killed both the lion and the bear; this uncircumcised Philistine will be like one of them, because he has defied the armies of the living God. The Lord who rescued me from the paw of the lion and the paw of the bear will rescue me from the hand of this Philistine. (1 Samuel 17:34b–37)

Goliath sized David up as "little more than a boy" (1 Samuel 17:42), but that boy had already killed at least two of the fiercest wild animals who walked the earth and did so by grabbing their fur and beating them to death. Most likely, David had also developed lethal aim with his sling. He would soon go on to become a high-ranking army official, earning recognition for slaying "tens of thousands" (1 Samuel 18:7). And while David defeated Goliath because David invited God to work through him, there is no indication that God superseded David's gifts as he did so; as far as we can tell, God worked through them. God equips the called, and he also calls the equipped.

God promises to do the same for us. The leader of the Christian organization I mentioned lacked the typical experience of someone in his role. Still, why did the board offer him the job? Undoubtedly, because they felt he possessed the gifts to serve as an effective leader. That doesn't mean God deserves any less credit for the work he does through our gifts, because where do our gifts come from? All the good we do can be attributed to God. God desires to accomplish more through us than we may think is possible. But most likely, he will leverage the unique gifts he granted to us when he does so.

The Whole Truth

This chapter jumped on common half-truths Christians often believe when discerning God's calling. Two themes are key. The first is that discerning God's will for our work and lives requires wisdom and effort. The second suggests that discerning your calling with wisdom starts with your gifts. The role of our gifts in helping us understand where we are best suited to serve within the church is highlighted in Scripture, and the principle also applies to the world of work. Psychologists have developed reliable tools that can assist in this process. There is great wisdom in using these as part of a well-informed decision-making process, a process that is itself informed by what we know works in career decision-making and planning. This approach gets very practical very quickly, and it's where we turn next.

PART 2

Discerning Your Calling

CHAPTER 3

What Works in Career Decision-Making?

GABRIELLA WAS EAGER to come home for the weekend. A month ago, her parents helped her move into her dorm room and said their good-byes, leaving her to make her way as a newly (and finally!) independent first-year university student. She couldn't have been more excited. Yet when she looked around, she noticed that most other students seemed to have something she lacked: a clear plan. Two of her friends were engineering majors who had the next four years totally mapped out. Two others were premed; both of them, curiously, had a parent who was a physician, so they knew what they were facing. Gabriella's roommate was an art major who fit the free-spirited stereotype; her path seemed tailor-made for her. When Gabriella looked at her own future, all she saw was uncertainty. She had no idea what she wanted to do with her life. Whenever she thought about it, anxiety surged through her body. *How do I figure out what God is calling me to do?* she wondered. Her parents were a steady source of support, and she longed for their advice and encouragement.

Gabriella didn't realize, however, that during the short month since she started school, life had quickly changed for her parents. Her dad, Alejandro, worked in manufacturing his entire career, but his company announced a wave of layoffs, and his name was among the unfortunate group who would need to find other employment. His wife, Marci, continued to bring in a steady but small paycheck as a librarian. Alejandro knew that when his severance payments stopped at the end of the year, he'd feel pressure to find another job, sooner rather than later. But what kind of job? There did not seem to be any similar positions in manufacturing anywhere near their home. Some retooling at least, and maybe a complete change of direction, seemed imminent. He found himself asking the same question as his daughter: *How do I figure out what God is calling me to do?* He looked forward to offering support for Gabriella when she arrived that weekend, but he'd be doing so from a position of fresh vulnerability.

Gabriella and Alejandro occupied two very different stages in life, but their questions and needs were suddenly very similar. Both faced an uncertain future, both yearned for a sense of direction, and both wanted to know a good way to discern God's calling for their careers. This chapter addresses these concerns.

The Practice of Discerning a Calling

The needs experienced by Gabriella and Alejandro are familiar to me, because I experienced my own version of those same concerns firsthand, as I described earlier. Like Gabriella and Alejandro, I asked myself, *How do I figure out what God is calling me to do?* Sometimes I am asked what advice I would give the nineteen-year-old me, if I could travel back in time to the days when I was in those prayer rooms, pleading so intently for God to reveal his will. I'd have plenty of advice—like stop overthinking and overspiritualizing everything—but part of what I'd say is (1) to keep praying, but pray for the right things, and (2) to get active.

"Fine," nineteen-year-old me would reply. "But what are the

'right things' I should pray for, and what exactly does 'get active' mean?"

Most likely I would have wanted a series of steps—some clear objectives to carry out. For Christians, those steps begin with prayer and other spiritual practices, and they also include an active process that leverages what we know helps in career decision-making. Let's explore each of these in turn.

Pray for the Right Things: Spiritual Practices for Discernment

Since the early days of the church, Christians have engaged in spiritual practices to help maintain a posture of openness to God and a willingness to surrender to his will. What follows are some of the practices that have proven particularly helpful over the millennia, and that I've found personally helpful—not because they promise to reveal a particular path forward on their own but because they create the conditions in which wise discernment occurs.

Solitude and silence. Solitude means being alone, setting aside time specifically for communing with God, free from the clutter, distractions, and strivings that bombard our everyday lives. Solitude helps with being still and knowing that God is God (Psalm 46:10). With that as the goal, silence helps deepen the experience of solitude, freeing us from literal noise in our environment, and from figurative noise as well—our own thoughts bouncing around in our heads. How can you experience solitude and silence? That depends on your life circumstances and access to space in which solitude is possible. It may mean setting your alarm thirty minutes earlier and rolling out of bed before anyone else does or plugging alone time into your weekly schedule and protecting those slots like you would an important meeting. Regardless of when it occurs, it also means finding physical space where you can be alone and where your distractions are minimized. Maybe that means retreating to an unused room at your workplace, taking your lunch break outdoors, or investing in a decent pair of noise-cancelling headphones. It may not be easy at first and may require some trial and error, but the key is to find a system that works for you and to ensure it happens regularly.

At the start of each solitude session, get into a comfortable position, breathe deeply to calm your body, and pray that God will purge your mind of interruptions. Solitude and silence are at the heart of spiritual practices in many religious traditions, but for Christians the goal is not to "empty the self." Rather, it is to create space for focusing attention on God.

Deep reading of Scripture. During times of solitude it is easier to read Scripture in ways that foster spiritual transformation. A transformative approach to consuming the text means going beyond reading for the purpose of learning about history or familiarizing ourselves with Bible stories—although these are good things too. Instead, it involves placing ourselves within God's story, striving to understand our own identities in light of God's work of redemption articulated in the text. Chapter 1 and the appendix of this book address this in broad strokes, exploring how we can find our place within the frame of the Bible's Four-Act Story. That's important, but developing a deep openness and sensitivity to God's voice means also making regular practice of carefully and deliberately reading Scripture. It means dwelling on words or phrases that jump out at us or speak to us in a special way.[35] Doing this helps us take refreshment in God's presence and allows our hearts to respond in prayer as we meditate on each word and phrase.

Prayer. Our ability to discern is enhanced when we commune with God regularly through prayer. Prayer is expansive; all the ways we connect with God are encompassed in prayer. Yet how should we pray when we are praying for discernment? This is where the nineteen-year-old me was getting things wrong, when I regularly pleaded, "Lord, show me what you would like me to do, and I will do it," then waited for my moment of spiritual insight to arrive. The reality is that while God does call us to particular areas of work, most often he does so indirectly rather than directly. A good starting point in prayer for discernment, then, is to submit ourselves to God by placing our trust in him, asking for freedom from our competing desires, and seeking wisdom.

Responding to these goals of submitting to God and seeking wisdom, spiritual director and author Ruth Haley Barton suggests three types of discerning prayer I have found helpful.[36] The first is a simple *prayer of quiet trust*. Like the Psalmist, we can lift up to God our complete and total dependence on him, knowing he is in control of all things, including "great matters or things too wonderful for me" (Psalm 131:1b). This prayer can be very simple: "Lord, I place my trust in you." A second type of discerning prayer is the *prayer for indifference*. The prayer here is for God to work within our hearts to make us indifferent to anything but his will. Barton points out two examples in the Gospel of Luke: Mary's response upon learning she would give birth to the Messiah ("I am the Lord's servant. May your word to me be fulfilled" [1:38]), and Jesus's heart-wrenching prayer in the garden of Gethsemane. There he laid bare his desire to be freed from the brutal death he was staring in the face ("Father, if you are willing, take this cup away from me") before grounding himself in his Father's will: "Yet not my will, but yours be done" (22:42). The prayer for indifference reminds us to share our hopes, but to make them always subservient to God's will.

Once we have prayed for quiet trust and indifference to anything other than God's will, we can engage in *prayer for wisdom*. I discussed in chapter 2 how God has a specific plan for our lives but doesn't expect us to figure out every detail regarding what to do next before we decide. Instead, he gives us the freedom to make informed choices with wisdom. Rather than praying for a revelation, therefore, we can pray for wisdom. Scripture assures us that when we do, God won't hold back: "If any of you lacks wisdom, you should ask God, who gives generously to all without finding fault, and it will be given to you" (James 1:5).

Self-knowledge and self-examination. Discernment also requires growth in our self-understanding—our knowledge of what makes us unique, our strengths and liabilities, and our internal obstacles that may get in the way of our discernment. When we reflect on our attitudes toward our careers, sometimes we might notice our motives reflect values the world imposes on us, things that often do not reflect God's values. Perhaps we feel an internalized pressure to seek out the highest-paying job we can find, regardless of other considerations. Or perhaps we find ourselves prioritizing power or prestige, even if that means compromising our other callings in life. We may notice that we feel drawn to a particular career path because it would make other people happy more so than God, as was the case for Nate in the last chapter. A lot of practices are available that foster self-knowledge, and I introduce some shortly.

Before we continue, though, I feel compelled to convey one last point regarding spiritual practices for discernment. In the last chapter I noted that discerning a calling is not a onetime event, but rather an ongoing process. The same can be said about all discernment for Christians. All of us experience transition points in our lives, when our circumstances point to a need to make a major life decision, maybe involving a relationship, a course of study, or a job. Discernment is critical during times like these. But discernment is critical during all the other times too. Part of living a life of discipleship means *always* maintaining a posture of openness to God's will, and a willingness to surrender our will to his. For this reason, think of the practices in this section as habits you can cultivate all the time, on a daily basis, rather than only as needed.

Get Active: Clear Steps to Help Discern Your Career

Vocational psychology researchers often conduct experiments that compare outcomes for people with career concerns who participate in a career intervention to outcomes for people experiencing similar concerns who do not. By "intervention" here, I mean any kind of guided strategy or activity designed to help people address their career decision-making concerns. A large number of these experiments have accumulated over the years—so many that researchers have conducted several meta-analyses,[37] or studies of studies, on the question of what works in career interventions. In one landmark meta-analysis of sixty-two experiments with 7,725 participants,[38] Loyola University Chicago researchers Steve Brown and Nancy Ryan Krane investigated two questions: First, are career interventions effective? And second, if some interventions are more effective than others, what do the really helpful interventions include that the less helpful ones leave out?

The answer to that first question was a resounding yes: People with career concerns who participate in career interventions do indeed experience better outcomes than control group participants. In exploring the second question, Brown and Ryan Krane discovered that some combination of five specific components tended to show up in the most effective interventions. These "critical ingredients" are as follows: (1) written goal-setting and reflection exercises, (2) individualized interpretation and feedback, (3) information about the world of work, (4) support-building by enlisting encouragement and help from important people in participants' lives, and (5) modeling of effective career decision-making behavior.[39] So, what does it mean to "get active" in one's career decision-making? It means trying out these five critical ingredients.[40]

1. Write about your discernment process and set smarter goals. One way to make progress in career decision-making is to spend focused time writing out your thoughts and feelings about your career direction, especially your career goals. In psychology, a lot of evidence supports the power of expressive writing in helping people deal with challenges. Social psychologist James Pennebaker has studied for more than thirty years the psychological impact of writing personal narratives. Typically, his studies invite people to write about emotionally upsetting life events for brief periods of time (usually twenty minutes, without stopping) once per day over the course of a few days. Incredibly, he and his colleagues have found that engaging in this kind of writing is linked to enormous benefits, including improved immune system functioning, fewer health problems, better adjustment to college, and reduced time needed to find employment after being laid off.[41]

Pennebaker's work on writing to cope with traumatic events got Laura King thinking. A personality and social psychologist, she wondered if the benefits of writing extended beyond dealing with traumatic events. Would writing about priorities and goals in life have a similar impact on well-being, and even physical health? To test this possibility, King adapted Pennebaker's approach by asking participants to write for twenty minutes a day, for four consecutive days, about their "best possible future self." Most people find that something about a focused session of putting pen to paper (or typing on a screen) forces them to articulate their thoughts in a different, perhaps deeper, way than when they speak or think. The task doesn't require pie-in-the-sky dreams to offer benefit, either. Consider this response from King's study:

> I guess . . . I want a pretty normal middle-class life. I want just a medium-size house—no mansions even if I could afford it. . . . My main goal is to keep experiencing as much as I can; even when It seems there isn't anything else, there always is. Really, I just want a good marriage, where we are both confident together and complement each other's personalities. Once we are happy together we could be happy in lots of different situations—even if it means some sacrifice. My ideal would be for us both to love, or at least be proud of, our jobs, but also always strive for more.

This paragraph was typical of respondents, expressing aspirations to a "normal" existence, a strong marriage, and jobs they can be proud of, even if they aren't jobs they always love. Across all participants, common themes included a successful career, personal growth, marriage and family, travel, and home ownership. What were the effects of this kind of writing? When she followed up with participants five months later, King found that writing about a positive future, and the goals required to get there, led to significant gains in happiness and life satisfaction, and also fewer doctors' visits, compared to people in a control condition.[42] Try expressive writing yourself, using a slightly adapted version of the instructions that King used:

Think about your career in the future. Imagine that
everything has gone as well as it possibly could. You
have worked hard and succeeded at accomplishing all
of your career goals. Think of this as the fulfillment of
your calling. Now, write about what you have imagined.

In Brown and Ryan Krane's meta-analysis, the writing exercises deployed by those super-effective career interventions
included writing in journals, diaries, logs, and workbooks.[43]
One of the dominant themes embedded in many of these written exercises was the importance of establishing career goals
and planning how to implement them. Goals are a powerful
influence on behavior; they help us organize our activity and
pursue a particular target with purpose. Yet people struggle with
setting goals; just 25 percent of adults have clear goals for where
they want to be in five years.[44] In general, research suggests that
both pursuing and achieving goals boosts happiness, and writing goals down is even more powerful than thinking or talking
about them; it creates a kind of psychological contract for people with themselves. That's especially true when people set their
own goals rather than follow goals that others suggest for them.

If you are grappling with a discernment process right now,
give written goal-setting a try. Write down five goals that you are
pursuing in your career path right now. Are they effective goals?
A good way to evaluate your goals uses the acronym SMARTER.[45]
Strive for these seven principles when setting a goal:

1–2. A smarter goal is *Specific* and *Measurable*. "To feel better about where my career is headed, as soon as possible"
may speak to a pain point, but it's neither specific nor
easily measurable. "Within the next month, interview

three people who work in a career path that is exciting to me" is clear, measurable, and a far more effective goal.

3. A smarter goal is challenging, but *Attainable*. It may require some effort to pursue, but if you expend that effort, you can achieve the goal. Climbing Mount Everest next week is a challenging but unattainable goal.[46] "Complete a battery of career assessments before Friday" or "By tomorrow, schedule a visit with a mentor"— these are attainable.

4. A smarter goal is *Relevant* to your larger objective. If that larger objective is, say, deciding on a college major or identifying a new career path to pursue, work backward from there to identify goals that will bring you closer to the desired endpoint. For example, "Within the next week, gather detailed information about training requirements for three promising career paths" is a highly relevant goal.

5. A smarter goal is *Time-bound*. Open-ended goals are less likely to drive success than goals with target dates. If you hope to have clarity in your career by year's end, treat it like a deadline and work out a timeline for each goal leading up to it.

6. A smarter goal is one for which you are fully *Engaged*. You are setting your own goals here; choose ones you are highly motivated to carry out, because you'll need that kind of full engagement when you face the inevitable obstacles.

7. Finally, a smarter goal is one for which you receive *Reinforcement*. The best kind of reinforcement involves support and encouragement, but also feedback to help you evaluate your progress and make adjustments where

necessary. You can use self-reinforcement (e.g., "I have interviewed two of the three people I said I'd interview this month, and it's gone well. I can do this. Just one more to go!"). But involving the help and support of others, both for encouragement and accountability, makes reaching your goals all the more likely. More on this shortly.

Writing about your career concerns and writing down goals are actions you can take to find clarity. Doing these things will help you articulate your developing sense of calling and may relieve some of your stress too.

2. Seek out individualized interpretation and feedback. There are general steps that everyone can follow to discern a calling, but the particular elements within each step require attending to what makes you unique. That's why interventions that include individually tailored feedback are more effective than those with a one-size-fits-all approach. This is the "critical ingredient" that most directly harnesses the biblical principle that people have different gifts, and understanding those gifts is important for discerning a calling. Some effective interventions in Brown and Ryan Krane's meta-analysis gave individually tailored feedback on papers written about career plans, a nice tie-in to the previous critical ingredient of written exercises. The most common source of individualized interpretive information in these interventions, though, comes in the form of career assessments.

Assessments offer an efficient way for people to learn more about themselves. If you had unlimited time, maybe you could sample different lines of work until you found one that fit you well. Maybe someone has even advised you to try this! While nothing replaces real-world experience, you don't have unlimited time, and many logistical challenges come with the trial-and-error approach. Assessments offer the next best thing. They provide a way to learn about the kind of general tendencies you exhibit that influence whether you are a good fit for a particular job. Career assessments are designed to translate an abstract concept, like career interests, work values, or personality, into a measurable unit. That usually involves responding to a series of items that ask you to choose an option that best reflects a current preference or attitude. Your item responses are combined to generate a score profile, and interpretive feedback is presented alongside your scores to describe how you differ from other people and what you might expect from various opportunities in the world of work, based on what is typical for people with your pattern of scores. Assessments that carry out this process well offer insight into your unique qualities.

A word of caution, however. It is essential to use scientifically supported career assessments, because all assessments are not created equal. Far too many of them apply flawed and poorly evaluated methods to generate scores. Their score profiles may look attractive, and they may be marketed well, but some of these assessments are dangerous because they provide invalid information. Making decisions with long-term consequences based on bad information is a recipe for disappointment, frustration, and maybe disaster. For this reason, Googling "career test" and taking the first free online questionnaires that show up is not a good strategy.[47] In the next two chapters, I invite you to complete a series of career assessments as part of PathwayU, which have been developed and refined using years of rigorous scale development research.

The broader point here is the recommendation to use individualized interpretation and feedback, derived from high-quality sources of information, to develop a better sense of what makes you unique—your "gifts." We explore this in much greater detail in chapter 4.

3. **Leverage in-depth world-of-work information.** Once you have a clearer sense of your gifts, the next step is to consider how those gifts make you well-suited for particular opportunities. That is not easy to do, however, without access to accurate and up-to-date information about your options. As a starting point, when exploring career paths, most people are advised to consider at least the following: interests and values that are typically satisfied by an occupation, typical work activities, training requirements, opportunities there may be to advance, salary data and earning potential, and an occupation's economic outlook (i.e., whether the number of jobs in that occupation is expected to grow, shrink, or remain steady). This is a lot of information to digest, but gathering it helps form the basis of informed decision-making.

One source of information available online is the Occupational Information Network (O*NET), a database maintained by the U.S. Department of Labor. The O*NET is searchable and offers extensive and detailed information about roughly a thousand different occupations. It is the most extensive database of occupational information available in the world, and it is free to use at www.onetonline.org. The O*NET is the result of decades of research on occupations and is supported by regularly updated economic data collected by the U.S. Bureau of Labor Statistics. If you want to know whether cartography has a bright outlook, what unique pattern of high and low interests is typical of happily employed auto body repair workers, or what credentials are needed to obtain an interior design job, you'll find all that on the O*NET. However, its comprehensiveness comes at a bit of a cost; the sheer volume of information the

O*NET provides can be overwhelming. As we explore in chapter 5, PathwayU curates O*NET information, packaging it into an easier-to-navigate form, while still granting access to the full array of information for users who want a deeper look.

For richer and more personalized details, informational interviews are very helpful. An *informational interview* is a brief, usually informal conversation you can have with someone for the purpose of gathering insight about a particular career field. It begins by identifying people who work in the career field about which you'd like to learn more. Depending on the occupation, you may know some eligible candidates already, but others will be strangers. Either way, push yourself to invite these folks to meet with you individually for a half hour or so. At that meeting, you can simply work through a list of interview questions you've prepared in advance (see chapter 5 for an example), questions that will give you an insider's perspective on a particular occupation. While it may require courage to arrange these meetings, they are almost always a positive experience and provide valuable insights on what a job is really like.

4. **Learn from role models** and 5. **Lean on your supports.** The last two critical ingredients in effective career interventions overlap. Modeling in career interventions involves learning decision-making strategies from people who have gone before you and had success doing so. Attention to support-building recognizes that career decisions are best made with the help of friends, family, and mentors who can provide advice and encouragement. Modeling and support-building both converge with the Bible's teachings on the role of discipleship in fostering spiritual formation, which draw from an ample supply of mentoring examples—for example, Moses and Joshua, Naomi and Ruth, Elijah and Elisha, Jesus and his disciples, Paul and Timothy.

Vocational psychology theory and research suggest that few

influences can boost a person's decision-making confidence more than learning from role models.[48] Think about it— whenever you want to build confidence in a particular skill, it always helps to seek out people who have mastered that skill and learn from them. The studies in Brown and Ryan Krane's meta-analysis that included modeling exposed participants to people who had already achieved success in exploring careers, deciding, and obtaining a position within their chosen field. Especially when you personally identify with the people you are learning from, hearing others share about their experience can have a big impact.

Knowing this effect for modeling, I once conducted an experiment to see if modeling in the form of counselor self-disclosure could help participants discern a calling.[49] In this study, my colleague Michael Steger and I designed a brief workshop intended to assist students with making decisions about their career paths. We divided workshop participants into two groups. With the first group, we asked the counselor leading the workshop to share her own personal story about how she discerned her calling. With the second group, we asked her to use hypothetical examples (e.g., "Imagine there is a person who . . . "). When we compared the two groups, we found that the students who had listened to the counselor share her personal story reported greater confidence in their ability to manage the decision-making process, and also a stronger sense of meaning in life, than the group who heard the hypothetical examples. The activities participants completed during the workshop sessions were the same, but learning from someone who had personally navigated the process herself boosted their confidence and left them with a stronger sense of purpose as they looked ahead.

What does this mean for you? You should seek out role models and cling to them (figuratively, please), because what you can learn from a role model is powerful. Use your network to identify someone who is living a calling in a career about which you'd like to know more. Seek out people like this boldly and ask them to share with you how they achieved what they did. If they can do it, you probably can too.

Beyond modeling, support is powerful. Support boosts one's confidence but also helps a person move from making plans to actually taking steps to make those plans happen. Some of the most effective interventions that Brown and Ryan Krane identified in their meta-analysis focused on enlisting help and support from families and friends. Some interventions also brought in support from people who understood the cultural contexts in which participants lived—people who could teach them how to interact in positive ways with their environments. This fits with other research that found that support from friends and family has a huge impact on the careers young people aspire to, that a lack of support from peers can limit their aspirations, and that support helps youth successfully transition into the world of work.[50] Career decisions are never permanent, but neither are they trivial; they are big decisions. And big decisions are more wisely made within the context of support, rather than in a vacuum.

Within your own life, who can you count on for encouragement, support, wisdom, and a healthy dose of perspective? These people are your *circle of support*. Often, it helps to establish a mechanism for leaning on their support in an intentional way as you go through the discernment process. Start by naming people who make up two separate (but likely overlapping) circles, one consisting of people who serve as wise advisers, and the other consisting of people who serve as support-giving encouragers. You might call the first group your Personal Board of Advisers and the second group your Personal Board of Encouragers. Who can you invite to serve in each of these groups? Seriously, write these names down right now. When identifying your circles of support, consider the following tips:

- *List at least three people in each group.* Diverse viewpoints from people who know you in different contexts are valuable. Collectively, they offer a more well-rounded perspective than what is possible from just one or two people. When you see areas of convergence, or themes that cut across what you hear from these folks, pay special attention.
- *Do not include someone with an agenda.* We all know people who have a strong, sometimes self-serving, opinion about what we "should" do with our lives, and who seem more eager to express that opinion than listen carefully to our concerns. Take the advice of such people lightly, and balance it with other perspectives you trust.
- *Lean especially on people you trust.* These are people who care about you; you have known a long time; are wise; have substantial life experience; share your values, especially your faith; are kindhearted; are good listeners; and are encouraging.

After you've named these people, contact each of them and share that you are currently engaged in a discernment process and could use their help. This may feel unnatural or awkward but take courage and speak from the heart. Most likely, they will feel honored by your request and will happily offer their assistance. For members of your Board of Advisers, ask if they are willing to connect with you for a short one-on-one meeting. During that meeting, tell your story and ask for feedback and advice, using questions such as:

- How on track do I seem right now?
- What should I be asking myself that I don't seem to be at the moment?
- What do you see as my strengths?
- What seem like promising pathways for me?

Take a notebook and jot down your thoughts as you have this conversation. For members of your Board of Encouragers, ask if they'd be willing to provide a listening ear and support when needed. Tell your story to them, too—freely express your concerns and lean on their encouragement for strength and persistence. Discerning a calling is not easy, but it is much easier when others are walking alongside you.

The Ongoing Process of Discernment

Gabriella and Alejandro both faced a period of discernment and both needed to make some key decisions about their career paths. This chapter outlined evidence-based strategies for carrying out this process. If Gabriella and Alejandro both commit themselves to spiritual discernment practices such as solitude and silence, deep reading of Scripture, and prayer, they will likely maintain the spiritual posture of openness they need to support the discernment process. If they build on these practices by "getting active," fearlessly engaging in discernment practices aimed at better understanding themselves and the world— practices such as completing written exercises, seeking individualized interpretation and feedback, gathering accurate and up-to-date occupational information, leaning on role models, and soaking up support—the answers to their questions regarding what they ought to do next will soon emerge.

Even so, as I've already discussed, a calling is not a thing to be discovered once and for all. Living a calling is a dynamic, continually unfolding process. Discerning a calling doesn't end when a person decides on a career path—that is only the beginning. Integrating faith with work is a way of cocreating in divine partnership and serving as a "minister of reconciliation" to restore order and goodness (i.e., shalom) within whatever career path God calls you to. Doing so requires staying active in the discernment process on an ongoing basis and continually listening for God's voice as communicated in Scripture and through his creation. It also requires a better understanding of how you can express your God-given gifts in your career. It is to that topic—understanding and applying your gifts—that I turn to next.

CHAPTER 4

Your Gifts, and the Difference They Make

I LOVE COFFEE SHOPS. *Love* them. For many reasons. I love hearing the crackling rumble of grinding beans, the hissing whistle of frothing milk, and the quiet buzz of a dozen conversations competing with Miles Davis or Diana Krall pouring softly out of the speakers. I love the pungent fragrance of coffee oils wafting through the space, covering me like a weighted blanket when I walk in. I love the way the right kind of coffee shop makes me instantly feel creative, motivated, eager to just get stuff done. But most of all, I love how coffee shops function as a sort of unofficial community center, a meeting place where people from all walks of life gather, often to work on whatever they need to do. On a typical Tuesday, I might see an attorney cranking on a brief in one corner; a group of nurses in scrubs chatting about their shifts in another; newlyweds mulling over photo packages with a young photographer; a composer wearing headphones, crafting a score on a laptop; and a workboot-clad cluster of contractors gathered around a conference table, scrolling through a series of drawings and making plans for the next morning. I marvel at the diversity of gifts on display in this one place—a microcosm of what is happening throughout my community and elsewhere. To me, it speaks of God's handiwork, our social fabric woven in such a way that we have lots of interconnected needs, but also lots of people well-equipped to address those needs.

In chapter 2, I argued that a key strategy for discerning a calling is learning about your gifts and identifying career paths that fit them well. In chapter 3, I noted that this strategy (via individualized interpretation and feedback, and access to occupational information) is embedded in the critical ingredients that comprise the most effective career interventions. This way of understanding how gifts function is also rooted in Scripture's teachings[51] about spiritual gifts, or special abilities given by the Holy Spirit to believers for the purpose of building up the body of Christ. The questions of what makes us unique and where we are best equipped to serve are relevant not only in the church but in the world of work as well. For that reason, when discerning our callings in the world broadly, we are free to consider our gifts broadly as well. This means expanding our field of vision beyond the spiritual gifts specifically mentioned in Scripture and looking at what scholars have identified as relevant gifts within the world of work.

Gifts, Career Paths, and the Common Good

What core dimensions of "gifts" are the ones you should consider? Vocational psychologists usually point to four: interests, values, personality, and abilities. To take inventory of your gifts, go to PathwayU (redeemingwork.pathwayu.com), create a profile, complete the assessments, and read through your results. Then read what follows in this book with your scores in mind. After discussing your gifts in this chapter, I explore how they translate to particular career paths in the next.

Jayla completed these assessments and serves here as an example to illustrate these areas of gifts. Jayla considers herself a "starving artist," surviving on proceeds from jewelry she makes and sells at craft shows and online through Etsy. She loves the creative parts of her work. "I feel so much joy when I'm working on a new project," she says, "like God is smiling on me." Unfortunately, Jayla has struggled to earn a livable wage. She gets by because her expenses are low—she is single and shares an apartment with two roommates—but feels strongly she'll need to do something else soon. Most likely, she'll keep her jewelry business going on the side (because she loves it!) while pursuing a calling within a different career full-time. But what career? Her interests, values, personality, and abilities can help her identify a promising path forward.

Interests

Interests refer to things (e.g., activities, school subjects, types of people, leisure pursuits) you enjoy. Formally, interests are stable dispositions that draw people toward particular sets of activities. Vocational psychologist Bruce Walsh put it more simply when he described interests as "motivations that determine life decisions."[52] What kinds of school subjects or work tasks have you always (or never) enjoyed? When you are working, pay attention to those moments when you love your job the most—when you lose track of time because you are fully absorbed in what you are doing. What exactly are you working on during those moments? Alternatively, what kinds of things do you like to do for fun in your downtime? Your answers to these questions reflect your interests and are part of what make you uniquely "you."

In 1943, Stanford psychology professor E. K. Strong Jr.[53] used a boat analogy to describe how interests interact with other personal characteristics as a person's career unfolds: "The relationship among abilities, interests, and achievements may be likened to a motor boat with a motor and a rudder. The motor (abilities) determines how fast the boat can go, the rudder (interests) determines which way the boat goes."[54] By the time he wrote those words, Strong had investigated interests in dozens of pioneering research studies, including several that tracked people over time—some over more than two decades. He found that scores on interest inventories tended to change very little, on average, even over that amount of time. This evidence of stability is supported by more recent research as well and suggests that assessing your interests now offers valuable information for informing potentially long-term career decisions.[55] Furthermore, in a comprehensive review of hundreds of studies conducted since Strong's research, psychologists Phillip Ackerman and Eric Heggestad noted that, according to the evidence, "abilities, interest and personality develop in tandem, such that the ability level and personality dispositions determine the probability of success in a particular task domain, and interests determine the motivation to attempt the task."[56] This summary aligns completely with Strong's boat analogy, affirming the role of interests in guiding a person's motivation for pursuing a particular path. Your personality and abilities will influence how successful you might be within a path, but none of that matters if you don't start with a strong interest.

The most popular way of understanding interests comes from the late vocational psychologist John L. Holland.[57] Holland proposed that people and work environments can both be characterized according to six broad vocational types, which form the acronym RIASEC. Read their descriptions, and circle or highlight the ones you think are most characteristic of you.

- *Realistic.* People with *realistic* interests enjoy mechanical activities, athletics, working with their hands, being outdoors, and getting dirt under their fingernails.
- *Investigative.* People with *investigative* interests enjoy ask-

ing intellectual questions and investigating the answers
to those questions, maybe using the methods of science.
- *Artistic.* Those with *artistic* interests really appreciate self-
expression, certainly through fine arts but also through
drama, writing, music, and even culinary activities.
- *Social.* People with *social* interests like being in roles
where they can directly help people—teachers, pastors,
and counselors, for example.
- *Enterprising.* Those with *enterprising* interests enjoy per-
suading people. They do so in business-related tasks like
sales and marketing, but also through law, politics, and
public speaking.
- *Conventional.* People with *conventional* interests enjoy
organizing things. They love detail-oriented tasks and get
a kick out of things like filing systems and spreadsheets.

Note that people don't just have one type of interest; they usually have interests in all six domains, just to varying degrees.
(By the way, having an interest in something doesn't necessar-
ily imply having a related ability—someone can deeply enjoy
music, for example, without being able to carry a tune.) This
RIASEC model has been heavily investigated and repeatedly ver-
ified by research, and PathwayU offers a scientifically supported
inventory you can use to reliably determine your "Holland
code"—generally your highest three interest types.[58] Give it a
shot—take the assessment, see how you score, and compare it
to what you expected.

Keep in mind, there is a pattern in how the RIASEC types
are related. Look at Holland's famous RIASEC hexagon. The
hexagonal arrangement illustrates how similar the interest
types are to each other: those next to each other on the hexagon (R and I, or S and E, etc.) share substantial overlap; those

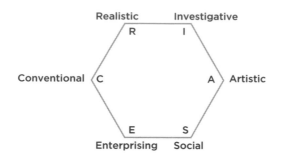

opposite each other (R and S, I and E, A and C) are the most dissimilar, and the alternating types (R and A, I and S, A and E, etc.) are somewhere in-between. If your "Holland code" consists of types in close proximity on the hexagon, you'll have an easier time making career decisions than someone with diametrically opposed types, partly because more career paths are available that satisfy your pattern of interests. For example, someone with strong realistic and investigative interests (next to each other on the hexagon) will notice that almost any engineering job satisfies that combination. In contrast, someone with conventional and artistic interests (types on opposite sides) will have to get creative to satisfy both in a job—maybe doing accounting work (satisfying conventional interests) for a local symphony (satisfying artistic interests) or forging a path as a studio artist (artistic) while meticulously organizing a system for storing paints and brushes (conventional). Often, people with this combination of interests work in a conventional job while pursuing artistic interests on the side.

Finally, the "shape" of your profile matters. People with one dominant interest type—a spike in their profile—usually have an easier time making decisions than do people with a "flat profile," in which several of their highest scores are very close to each other. In the case of a "high flat" profile (i.e., one with many high scores), a person may find herself having a hard time deciding on one pathway when several others look really appealing (this scenario describes my problem when I was a college student struggling to identify my calling). This profile presents a challenge, but it also means that person could derive satisfaction and meaning from a broad range of possible options. Of course, some people have lots of low interest scores. Sometimes that kind of "low flat" profile suggests the person was feeling kind of down, or was in a bit of a funk, when taking the assessment. Other times it simply conveys that the individual has a narrow range of interests; activities within that narrow range are exciting, but everything else is rated as low.

Jayla's highest interest score was artistic, by a large margin. Her conventional and investigative interests were both very low, and the other three—realistic, enterprising, and social—were all in the mid range. Jayla could see how her personal experience confirmed these results. Artistic interests, from designing jewelry to playing the lead in her high school musicals, are deeply rooted in her experience. She is not particularly well-organized (low conventional) and never loved her science classes (low investigative). However, she enjoys sports and being outside (realistic), likes to offer help to people who need it (social), and has started to enjoy most of the tasks involved in running her business (enterprising). Knowing her interests gave Jayla insight on what makes her unique and helped her realize that whatever she pursues next, opportunities for creative self-expression will need to be at the heart of it, while working with her hands, helping people, and engaging in business-related activities would be icing on the cake. She also recognized that her profile of scores fits her current gig pretty well, but she was curious about other opportunities her results identified.

Values

Whereas interests refer to what you enjoy, values refer to what you find important. Christians talk a lot about values—Christian values, biblical values, family values, and so on. All of these matter, but when it comes to the type of work that fits you best, it is critical to assess work values—the reinforcing conditions you want in your ideal career, without which you would likely feel frustrated and discontent. To experience joy, purpose, and meaning in your career, what do you most need in a work environment? Your answer reveals your work values. The best-supported work values framework[59] consists of six broad value dimensions. Read them, and while you do, make a note of the values that describe what you find most important at work:

- *Achievement.* People with *achievement* values want to do something that makes use of their abilities, and that gives them a sense of accomplishment.
- *Independence.* Those with *independence* values appreciate being able to plan their work with little supervision, try out their own ideas, and make decisions on their own.
- *Recognition.* People who value *recognition* want the opportunity to advance in a job, appreciate getting recognition for their work, like being viewed as "somebody" in the community, and seek out the authority to tell people what to do.
- *Relationships. Relationship* values are characteristic of people who desire supportive friendships with their coworkers, want to do things in service of others, and want to avoid being asked to do work they feel is morally wrong.
- *Working conditions.* People who value *working conditions* want to keep busy while at work, like variety on the job,

desire pay that compares well with that of other workers, and appreciate steady employment.

- *Support.* Those with *support* values want their organization to administer its policies fairly and desire supervisors who back up employees with upper management and who train workers well.

Work values are tricky to measure because people generally want it all in a job. The problem is, if a job that reinforces all of those values exists, I haven't seen it. No job has it all. This is why the best measures of values use a rank-ordering approach, forcing you to differentiate between values that are merely important and those that are absolutely a necessity. These non-negotiables are the values that, when satisfied, help you feel most like yourself. Give the values assessment included in PathwayU a try. What are your highest work values?

After identifying your values, the next step is to think about what career paths are most likely to satisfy them. Do you value relationships more than anything? If so, a job in which you are holed up in a quiet office, unable to interact much with other people, is going to make you miserable. Is independence one of your top values? If so, a highly structured job with strict rules for how the work should be done will feel suffocating. Jayla's top values were relationships and achievement, and her third-highest was working conditions. She reflected on how these scores fit her personal experience and realized the top two match her current gig well: she satisfies her relationship values through her connections with repeat customers and other makers who attend shows, and she satisfies her achievement values when she creates something she knows is beautiful and uses her business acumen to sell it. However, her working conditions value is not satisfied at all by her highly unpredictable (and usually low) monthly income. In her next career path, a more stable and sustainable situation will be essential, provided it still satisfies her relationship and achievement values.

Personality

Personality traits are consistent, enduring tendencies that reflect how you typically think, feel, and act over time and across situations. Identifying and describing your personality can help you evaluate whether a particular career path will allow you to "be who you are," like a swimmer gliding with the current rather than laboring against it. The most common way psychologists study personality traits is by asking people to rate themselves or others on a list of items, usually trait adjectives (like "talkative," "inventive," or "disorganized"). Then they analyze those ratings, gathered from large samples of people, using sophisticated statistical methods designed to identify groupings of items consistently linked to each other. Those groupings, or factors, tend to have common themes, and researchers label the factors accordingly. In carrying out this research over the last twenty years, personality scholars have observed a remarkably consistent pattern. Across many different languages and cultures all over the world, with many different samples of people rating both themselves and others, six broad personality factors continually emerge. These six traits are summarized using the acronym HEXACO,[60] and they are described below. As you did for interests and values, read these and consider whether you might score high, low, or somewhere in the middle on each of them.

- *Honesty-humility.* High scorers are often described as honest, fair, sincere, modest, and unassuming. They avoid taking credit even when it is deserved, and they are rarely tempted to break rules or manipulate people.

Low scorers really enjoy wealth and luxury and are often willing to flatter people to gain social status or special recognition. They come across as extremely confident and self-important and agree with the statement "Rules are made to be broken."

- *Emotional stability.* High scorers are calm, cool, and collected. They are relaxed, resilient, optimistic, and self-assured. Low scorers are often anxious, tense, and somewhat easily stressed. They tend to be pessimistic, moody, and sentimental.

- *eXtraversion.* High scorers are talkative, assertive, adventurous, social, spunky, and the life of the party. They often feel a rush of energy when around other people. Low scorers are reserved, introspective, and quiet; appreciate the chance to work independently; and enjoy spending time by themselves.

- *Agreeableness.* High scorers are cooperative, trusting, good-natured, compassionate, forgiving, and polite. They are harmonizers who steer clear of conflict and are generally pleasant to be around. Low scorers are cynical, stubborn, blunt, and competitive. They have strong opinions and are unafraid to share them, can get angry easily, and are often critical of others' shortcomings.

- *Conscientiousness.* High scorers are typically described as responsible, persevering, organized, disciplined, and determined. They are highly reliable, and employers usually love them. Low scorers are free-spirited, spontaneous, prone to distraction, and comfortable taking risks. They are highly flexible, but often struggle to follow through, and could benefit from extra accountability.

- *Openness to experience.* High scorers are creative, imaginative, bright, curious, open-minded, and witty. They thrive when creating new plans, tackling complexity, and innovating. They find new possibilities very exciting. Low scorers are down-to-earth, conventional, practical, and content with the familiar. They are better at implementing a plan than dreaming one up, and they strive for simplicity over complexity.

Keep in mind these are continuous traits, not "either/or" types. Take extraversion, for example. Research suggests that it is simply not true that a person is either an introvert or an extravert, as if there are only two options. Instead, some people score really high on extraversion, some people score really low, and most of us are somewhere between the extremes. The question is not, "Are you an introvert or an extravert?" but rather, "Where do you fall on the continuum of extraversion?" If you score right in the middle, it may mean you don't have a clear preference, or that it depends on the situation—some situations may evoke extraverted behavior in you, and others may activate introversion. This dimensional approach is how all six HEXACO traits operate.[61]

Jayla reflected on her personality patterns after seeing her scores. She scored very high on honesty-humility, agreeableness, and openness to experience; in the mid-range on conscientiousness and extraversion; and moderate to low on emotional stability. Given these scores, a creative career in which she has lots of relationships, but where she can occasionally take some time to herself, would probably feel like a natural fit. A low-conflict workplace that values collaboration more than competitiveness would be ideal, as would a high-trust environment. Jayla is working on her growth edges by engaging in self-care to manage her stress and by focusing more on her identity in Christ and less on how others evaluate her. While doing that, she wants to identify a career that will let her strengths shine—a path that will give her opportunities to express her creativity, to innovate and develop new skills, and to work with a team of people striving toward a common goal they all value. I explore ways to accomplish this in the next chapter.

Abilities

Abilities refer to a person's capacity to perform particular physical or mental tasks. Most ability tests measure a range of ability factors, like verbal ability, numerical reasoning, spatial ability, short-term memory, reaction time, and so on.[62] Each of these abilities is related to both general intelligence and more narrowly defined specific skills. People with a high level of a particular ability, in theory, could quickly develop the specific skills related to that ability, given proper training and practice. For example, if I had a high spatial ability and I took a drafting class, that underlying ability would help me quickly learn the specific skills I need to make (and analyze) blueprints and technical drawings. Many career counselors try to help people infer their abilities by carefully examining their past experiences, like their successes in school and at work. This strategy is efficient but not always accurate; research tells us that self-estimates are only weakly related to objectively measured abilities. Where our insights fall short, however, other people's observations of us can help fill in the gaps. For this reason, when thinking about your abilities, it always helps to talk with other people who know you well and consider how your self-understanding fits with what they have noticed in you.

For Jayla, creative tasks had always come naturally to her—obviously including crafting things with her hands, but also writing, acting, and even cooking. She can also communicate well and is persuasive when the situation calls for it, which is why she enjoyed competing on the debate team in high school, something a lot of the other theater kids did, too. She had struggled a bit with math-related tasks, although usually found ways to compensate; having a knack for learning software applications helps with that. Spatial tasks always felt easy to her, perhaps the result of her stereotype-defying obsession with Minecraft during high school. Other than average-range scores on math-related subtests, Jayla always excelled on standardized tests. She is a creative achiever, appreciates beauty, instinctively includes people, strives for harmony, and perseveres in the face of challenges. For some people, attending to abilities helps narrow their range of best-fitting options by ruling out pathways that require high levels of abilities they do not possess. For others, especially people with a low view of their abilities, identifying their clearest strengths helps expand the range of options to consider. As for Jayla, she is modest, but she knows that her abilities are likely sufficient for success in most any of the options that align with her interests and values.

What Are Your Gifts?

Gaining a clearer sense of your gifts helps you understand what makes you unique within the world of work and serves as a key prerequisite to evaluating the fit of particular career paths. Before advancing to that step, pause and summarize your gifts. PathwayU offers measures of your interests, values, and personality, and self-reflection and conversations with people you know can give you a reading on your abilities. After collecting this information and thinking about it carefully, complete the following statements, quickly and confidently:

- *Interests.* In terms of my interests, I am someone who . . .

- *Values.* For me to be satisfied at work, it is important that . . .
- *Personality.* Based on my personality traits, people experience me as . . .
- *Abilities.* The abilities that come most naturally to me are . . .

What themes do you notice when you articulate your gifts? Take a minute and imagine yourself living out a calling in a role that allows you to fully express your uniqueness in ways that glorify God and make the world better. Discerning a calling is often a messy process. No set of assessments and exercises can possibly tell you what you ought to do with your life, but such resources can serve as an important part of a well-informed, Spirit-guided decision-making process, one that builds on prayerful wisdom. The next step is to consider how those gifts align with opportunities and needs in the world.

CHAPTER 5

Evaluate, Specify, Clarify

FOR CHRIS, hitting the pause button felt like his only real option. He had already crossed the threshold of what he could tolerate in student debt and was still barely halfway to his degree. Chris was studying business and loved learning, but the thought of spending the rest of his life behind a desk in an office park somewhere made him feel trapped, like a caged bird. *Why am I doing this?* he wondered. Chris took a semester off to gather himself, planning—hoping, really—to return with renewed focus and a more exciting future career in mind.

While working as many shifts as he could at an REI store, Chris set up regular meetings with members of his inner circle—his pastor, a former coach, an aunt, and a couple of friends, all of them role models who offered advice and support. He also assessed his interests, values, and personality. The results affirmed some things he already knew about himself. For example, he valued independence and achievement, enjoyed leading people, and was highly conscientious. But his results also provided some insights he hadn't fully considered, like a very high score on realistic interests. Chris loved spending time outdoors and cared deeply about the environment's health, but he had never really entertained hands-on outdoor work as a legitimate career path, maybe because it never seemed "professional enough." When he prayed over his future, though, he found himself most inspired, at peace, and at home when he was in nature, away from the bustle. He began to fantasize about working outside as a full-time gig, but he didn't have a clear sense of his options and didn't want to drop out of school, either. He found himself at a crossroads, asking God, *What is my niche?*

In the discernment process, after learning about your gifts, the next step is to explore how those gifts align with opportunities and needs in the world of work—and to consider those options in light of your emerging sense of calling, and the Bible's Four-Act Story. This chapter walks through that process.

Evaluate Pathways That Fit You Well

Chris didn't have a clear sense of the full range of pathways available to him. He's not alone in this. All of us, when we evaluate our options, fail to consider lots of possibilities that we were simply never exposed to while growing up. Think about it. Where did you learn about the world of work? If you're like most people, you learned about it from your parents, your parents' friends, your friends' parents, people in your church and community, your teachers, a summer job, what you watched on TV, and so on. These sources gave many of us a good sampling of what jobs are out there, but far from a comprehensive one; the last edition of the U.S. Department of Labor's *Dictionary of Occupational Titles* contained nearly thirteen thousand! Before narrowing things down, take a renewed look at your options to ensure that you haven't automatically eliminated viable career paths you simply never considered.

Consult Your Career Matches

PathwayU includes a Career Match tool that maps your unique pattern of interests and values onto the roughly one thousand job titles that make up the O*NET. Your Career Match results show you a long list of those occupations, organized by how well your interests and values align with the interest and values profiles that best describe happily employed people within those career paths. Each of those job titles is linked to a massive amount of information about that occupation, such as what training is required, whether opportunities are growing or shrinking in that field, typical job duties, and average salaries. Selecting a job title gives you an at-a-glance summary of that occupation, while also inviting you to dive as deeply into the details as you like.

When looking at your Career Match results, keep a few things in mind. First, emphasize to yourself that your matches do *not* tell you what you "should" do with your career. They are a great source of scientifically supported insight to inform your decision-making process, but they are only one source, better considered as a useful starting point.

Second, don't worry too much about the rank order of your career matches. Your eighth-strongest match, for example, might be something you should consider more so than those ranked higher. Perhaps you already have some relevant training, or perhaps there are a lot of job openings in your area within that field. Your best strategy is to focus on learning from the matches listed as "Very Strong" or "Strong," regardless of their ranking. Even better, go to your View options and select "Careers by Subject Area" to examine the domains with the highest proportion of Very Strong matches.

Third, expect to find some surprises on your list. People usually find a few of their matches to be wild cards that raise their eyebrows or even offend them. But even with these matches, you can learn about yourself. Choose one of those job titles and look at the details of that occupation. What interests does it satisfy? What values does it reinforce? As a career counselor, I once worked with a client who was mortified that she matched well with being a librarian. Then I reminded her she worked at a Barnes and Noble, and suddenly librarian made more sense. Another client laughed because flight attendant was a very strong match, until we noted that she loved to travel and strongly valued opportunities to show hospitality. A useful question to ask when confronted with a strong match that doesn't seem appealing is, "What about this occupation makes it a match for my interests and values, and what can I learn from this?"

Curate Your List of Good Fits, and Look for Themes

The list of occupations that fit you well—both in the Career Match tool and, of course, in real life—might be long. Remember, for most of us, there is likely more than one right answer to the question of which career aligns with our calling, because callings transcend particular job titles. Before narrowing things down, take some time to consider all the recommendations you find appealing, especially those in the Very Strong or Strong categories. Start by making your own list of those good-fitting occupations that seem especially enticing to you, regardless of how much training is required, what it pays, how easy it would be to find a job in that field, or whether you have the skills needed to be successful in it right now. If an occupation in your suggested matches sounds appealing, just add it to your list. You can do this within the Career Match tool by selecting "Add to Favorites."

Why is making a list like this helpful? First, the list of appealing options almost always reveals some clear themes. For Chris, the top of his list was dominated by jobs like foresters, forest fire fighting and prevention supervisors, park naturalists, fish and game wardens, and general and operations managers. Most of these jobs happen in the great outdoors, and several involve leadership. All of them fit with Chris's experience and his realistic and enterprising interests. While he had never seriously considered an "outdoor career," he was now beginning to do so. Also, the thought of leading a team was energizing. Remember Jayla from the last chapter? She had a wide array of options on her list like dancers; makeup artists (theatrical and performance); and broadcast news analysts. She had never taken dance classes or done makeup for theater, and she rarely watched broadcast news. Even so, she noticed that those careers all involved creativity, self-expression, and public performance. Those themes brought to mind her experiences in theater and debate, and they reinforced that whatever pathway she pursues, satisfying her artistic interests and achievement values will be key. After you construct your list, read through each job title and make note of any themes that seem apparent. How well do these themes fit with what you noticed in the last chapter, when looking at your gifts? Undoubtedly, you will see some convergence.

Second, more often than not, when putting together their list, people find themselves drawn to two or three particular job titles that seem especially exciting—specific pathways they just can't stop considering. When that happens, it is worth your attention. Wildfires are a major concern in the western United States, where Chris grew up, so he was immediately drawn to forest fire fighting and prevention supervisors, although park naturalists and fish and game wardens captured his attention too. Jayla flagged two occupations from her list as worth a closer look: art directors and public relations specialists. She noticed that the work of art directors satisfies artistic and enterprising interests and independence and achievement values, and the work of public relations specialists satisfies enterprising, artistic, and social interests and those same values of independence and achievement. Neither job title aligned perfectly with her profile, but the overlap was substantial, and the required skills seemed right in her wheelhouse. Money was not a big motivator for Jayla, but she noticed that the salary for either of these job titles would support her more comfortably than her jewelry business does.

Gather Details and Keep Evaluating

Once you've identified a few occupations that jump out as particularly exciting, do what Chris and Jayla did: click on one of those job titles and dig into the details in the PathwayU Career Match tool. For each occupation, ask yourself:

- What in its description sounds especially interesting?
- What knowledge and skills are required?
- What training is needed, and how accessible is that to me?
- Are opportunities in this field expanding?
- Will I be able to support my family with a typical salary in this field?
- How plentiful are opportunities in this field in the region where I want to live?

The Career Match results summarize this information for each of your matches and connects you to greater detail in the O*NET (just hit the "Learn More" button). Your goal is to make an informed choice for your career path, so gather the details you need for a thorough evaluation of each potential opportunity.

As you learn more about the occupations you find most appealing, keep asking yourself how well a career in that field might satisfy your interests and values. Recall again Strong's boat analogy—your interests (and values) are the rudder that influences your direction, and your personality and abilities influence how fast and far you will go in that direction. With that in mind, as you gain clarity regarding how your interests and values are satisfied within those career paths, shift your attention toward personality and abilities. To facilitate this, complete the following sentences:

- The ways my personality traits could be an asset in this career include . . .
- My abilities would help me thrive in this career in the following ways . . .

Repeat this process with other career paths on your list. Evaluating the extent to which each job permits you to express your personality and abilities will help round out your view of how your gifts align with opportunities. To ensure you are doing this without obvious blind spots, use your assessment results from PathwayU and talk it through with people who can give you both support and honest feedback. Start with the people you named for your Personal Board of Advisers in chapter 3.

Conduct Informational Interviews

Once you've gathered detailed information about career paths that strike a chord with you, it will prove useful to dive even deeper in your information-gathering process. As noted in chapter 3, a good way to do this is to interview people who are currently working in the occupation about which you're trying to learn more. Informational interviews offer a chance to move beyond reading words on a screen to capturing a true insider's perspective, directly from a person intimately familiar with the line of work in question. Many people initially feel reluctant and uncomfortable when imagining carrying out an informational interview and are tempted to just skip over this step. But trust me: These interviews are extraordinarily helpful, so push through your discomfort. They need not be complicated, long, or intimidating. At their core, informational interviews are simply conversations.

An informational interview offers two key benefits. The first one is obvious: it gives you a view of what a career is really like from a person working in the trenches. The second is that it offers an initial step toward establishing a professional network within that occupation. People who enjoy their work tend to enjoy talking about it and may feel flattered by your interest in what they do. If you end up pursuing a career in that field down the road, that person may fondly remember you and provide assistance or connect you to others within the field who can offer help, as it is needed. This networking benefit should not be the primary reason you conduct such an interview, but it's a common, natural outcome of a positive interaction.

How do you arrange an informational interview? First, you must identify the right person—someone who works in the field in which you are interested and who is willing to talk with you. To accomplish this, start with people you already know; someone within your circle of friends and acquaintances may already be employed within the relevant occupation. If that's not the case, ask people you know if *they* have any connections in that field. An introduction from a mutual friend often takes the edge off any nervousness you might feel in anticipating the interaction. Still, if no one in your social circle can help you, don't worry. Instead, be bold and courageous, because those qualities will help you pursue your third option: cold-calling someone you haven't previously met. To identify who that might be, use online resources like LinkedIn to find people who have a particular job title, work for a particular employer, hold a particular degree, or belong to a particular professional network. Look for a person with whom you share something in common—maybe you went to the same school, lived in the same town, or have similar volunteer interests—because that can give you a good jumping-off point. Yet even if you make the request with no prior connection at all, don't be fearful; most people will be willing to help and will enjoy talking with you about their experience. As for the questions, choose six or seven that tap the details that most interest you. For example:

- How did you get started in this field?
- What does a typical day on the job look like?
- How does a typical career path unfold within this field?
- What have been the best, and worst, aspects of working in this occupation?
- What skills make or break someone in this line of work?
- What changes are occurring in this field, and how should a newcomer prepare for them?
- What advice do you have for someone thinking about entering this field?

Make sure to investigate your interviewee's background before the visit, so that you can ask specific questions about past experiences that look especially interesting or relevant.

Chris interviewed two members of a team of forest firefighters, one of whom supervised the crew. Chris was surprised to learn how much ongoing training is involved in the job, and while it seemed exciting and obviously goal-directed, he found the physical risks sobering. He also interviewed a park naturalist, and Chris loved the prevention and education aspects of the job. He wondered whether it would satisfy his interests in leadership and business, but he learned there were elements of the job that could involve marketing and leading teams, starting with teams of volunteers. That sounded really appealing to Chris. Jayla interviewed a public relations specialist who worked for a large tech firm in her area. The interview left Jayla unsettled; parts of managing a company's public image seemed exciting, but she wondered if the constant pressure might get to her. She also interviewed an art director who worked for a local advertising and media company. Jayla didn't use a lot of print media herself, but the creative aspects of ad layouts and banner designs seemed really fun to her.

Specify Your Pathway (a.k.a. Make a Choice)

You've now gone from consulting your career matches, to curating a list, to identifying themes, to gathering more detail (both electronically and ideally in person, using informational interviews). After all this, ask yourself: *How well would each of the occupations I'm considering permit me to use my gifts to glorify God and make the world better?* In answering this question, you may be drawn to one or two career paths that seem tailor-made for you. That was the case for both Chris (park naturalist) and Jayla (art director). If a career path with your name on it doesn't rise to the top right away, don't despair. Just keep gathering information; wise choices are informed choices. But at a certain point, you may find that multiple career paths seem to fit you equally well, and none are jumping out as the one path forward. Remember this point from chapter 2: multiple paths may align equally well with your calling. If this applies to you, take heart. A calling is broader than any one job, and if your gifts can be deployed well in more than one pathway, simply choose one of them and move forward.

That assurance was something I needed back when I agonized about God's calling for my career, concerned I might make the wrong choice. Sometimes people ask if I still feel I would have been faithful to my calling had I made a different choice, knowing what I know now. The answer is yes. My decision to apply to graduate school in psychology started the chain of events that ultimately led to the satisfying and meaningful career I have now. But would it have been tragic if I pursued sociology instead—or if I had gone straight into business, social work, or formal ministry? I don't think so. Any of those paths would have provided opportunities to express my gifts for God's glory. If I chose one of those other options, I would undoubtedly have ended up in a very different position. Still, I have every confidence that, with God's help, today I would have just as strong a sense of calling within that field that I have now in my current roles. I don't say this to convey that our choices don't matter, but rather to stress that we have freedom to make them, because callings are broader than any one job.[63]

Clarify Your Calling

It might seem strange to end this chapter with a charge to clarify your calling, and to do so *after* specifying a pathway to pursue. Yet as I hope is becoming clear, in the context of one's career, a calling is not a thing to be "found" or "discovered" once and for all, after which you ride off happily into the sunset. Rather, a calling is *built*. Discerning and living a calling are ongoing processes, a lifestyle of striving to serve faithfully while also looking for new ways to use your gifts within God's kingdom.

How would you describe your calling right now, as you reflect on your career up to this point and imagine where it is headed in the future? As Christians, our earnest prayer is for our life story to sync with God's larger story. That means orienting to the grand narrative of Scripture and embracing our role as Christ's ambassadors to other people and to the rest of creation. To clarify your calling, take the career path you're pursuing currently, or planning to enter, and ask yourself the following questions.

1. *What aspects of this area of work are rooted in God's creational design, and therefore need to be preserved, developed, and cultivated?*

This question recognizes the goodness of creation and of God's created intent. It calls your attention to where you see that goodness in your current or future area of work. This was an easy question for Chris: park naturalists organize experiences that help people better understand and appreciate the majesty of the natural world and encourage them to reflect on how they can better steward it. He saw the role as helping empower people to appreciate God's creation more deeply. Jayla viewed her work as taking what God made—raw materials but also fundamental principles of design—and using them to create more beauty.

A photographer may answer this question by pointing to God's glory in establishing how technology converges with the physics of light to capture images that tell the truth about the world and what is happening in it. A builder may answer it by marveling at the natural laws that infuse materials with their unique properties and govern how they can be combined in ways that form an attractive, functional building. Childcare providers may answer it by describing the optimism, hope, and potential they see in the children they serve. How would you answer this question for the occupation you're working in, or planning to pursue, right now?

2. *In what ways has this area of work been impacted by the fall, so that it now reflects a distortion of what God intended?*

The impact of sin takes many forms in different areas of work, and Christians are called to fight all of them. Chris sees this on a macro level, when governments or industries pursue policies that exploit rather than steward creation, and on a micro level, when he stops to pick up litter someone dumped on the side of a trail. Jayla sees exploitation in her field too, when designers manipulate images (like airbrushing waistlines of models) to sell falsehoods and promote distorted views of what beauty entails.

A supply chain manager might answer this question by identifying suppliers whose low costs or fast turnaround mask some serious cutting of corners, reducing product quality in potentially harmful ways, and hurting people along the way. An attorney might answer it by describing the blurred line between representing a client responsibly while also meeting the firm's expectations for generating billable hours. Members of marginalized groups might point to the systemic ways they face disadvantages in all sorts of career paths for reasons over which they have no control. How would you answer this question based on what you've experienced, observed, or expect in your career path?

3. *What would it look like for this area of work to be fully redeemed (that is, renewed), and what specific things can I do to work toward that?*

Your answer to this question may be very similar to your answer to the first. That's because to redeem means to "buy back," to restore—to cultivate and advance the goodness of creation to its best possible current state. While we long for that day when all things are made new, we also are called to help move our corner of creation in that direction. For Chris, park naturalists work to inspire people to preserve the wonder of creation by managing it responsibly, a goal that will only be fully realized when Christ returns but one that Chris can strive for today. For Jayla, full redemption for applied art means perfectly harnessing the raw potential in various media to help people think in new, different, and true ways about the world.

In her book *Kingdom Calling*, Amy Sherman unpacks Proverbs 11:10: "When the righteous prosper, the city rejoices."[64] It's a curious verse; one group prospers, and everyone in the city rejoices—really? More often, it seems like people become resentful when one group within a community prospers. But it helps to understand that the Hebrew term for "righteous" here is *tsaddiqim*, which refers to "the people who follow God's heart and ways and who see everything they have as gifts from God to be stewarded for his purposes."[65] The *tsaddiqim* place the needs of their community over their own needs, often at great personal sacrifice. So when they prosper, their focus on stewardship means that everyone in the community benefits. Sherman puts it this way: "As the *tsaddiqim* prosper, they steward everything—their money, vocational position and expertise, assets, resources, opportunities, education, relationships, social position, entrée and networks—for the *common good*, for the advancing of God's justice and shalom."[66]

As you write the story of your life and career, prayerfully consider how you can follow the example of the *tsaddiqim* and join Jesus in his work of making all things new. Don't worry if you don't have all the answers for what this looks like in your career right now. When embarking on a new career path, or planning a transition from one path to another, clarifying your calling simply means embracing and wrestling with the kinds of questions in this chapter, knowing that living out your faith in your career requires asking them over and over, and engaging your work accordingly. For most of us, the opportunity to do this requires actually finding a job. That quest is the focus of the next chapter.

CHAPTER 6

What Works in a Job Search?

THE YEAR Nick graduated from college, he decided to move to another state—not because he had a job lined up there, but because he wanted to live near his girlfriend, who was about to start graduate school. In the months leading up to the move, he started looking online for available jobs in the area. Nick was a psychology major and knew that he wanted to work with people in some way, but he didn't have a clear sense of what that might entail. He also didn't have a clear sense of how best to approach a job search. Without any contacts in what would become his new home, he mostly focused on scouring internet job boards to find anything that might fit. His first wave of effort didn't bear fruit.

After the move, Nick doubled down on his internet strategy, dedicating focused time each day to run searches, read job descriptions, tailor his cover letters and résumé, and submit application materials online. "Honestly, I didn't really know what I wanted," Nick recalls. "That summer, I mostly stayed behind a computer screen just cranking out application after application. It was exciting to do that—I would think, *It was a productive afternoon, I just submitted five applications!*—except that I would never hear anything back." He began to feel discouraged, and it was hard to stay motivated without getting so much as a nibble from prospective employers. He knew he had to adjust. "I started to realize that the people screening these applicants were bombarded with résumés. How would mine get their attention? Plus, I felt like it would be really hard for people to read my materials and see 'the real me' in them. I mean, my cover letter felt fake. Nothing about it was untrue, but it didn't capture who I really was. I just wished I could meet people so that they could get to know me." Nick prayed for these opportunities. "I knew that God knows who I am. He knows my strengths, and he's got a place for me in the world. I just wished God could go and explain who I am to these people so they would know I am a genuine person who really wants to work hard for them."

Nick eventually worked up the courage to try a more proactive strategy. He started submitting applications and then following up with a phone call. Sometimes he even drove to an organization's office and introduced himself to the hiring manager. "It was really intimidating to try and reach out to people like this," said Nick. "I had to really work to get myself out there. But this was kind of my gateway to formal networking." He started to see small signs of progress—e-mails from people he had met, thanking him for applying, and even an interview (albeit one that didn't materialize into an offer). Yet it still felt like an enormous amount of effort without a big return. The weeks turned into months. Nick felt humbled and frustrated. "My college built me up and sent me out there feeling like a shining star, but I soon realized it's not going to be handed to you. I was going to need to focus."

Nick took a job at a restaurant, which helped him pay his rent but also reinforced his need to find something that made use of his gifts. "At that point I had taken some assessments, and I started to realize a couple of things. First, it seemed like working in human resources would be ideal, given my strengths and the things I enjoyed the most. Training and development felt especially exciting—I could learn some things and then teach people, building them up and sending them back to their work with a new perspective and new skills. Second, it made me just so aware that I had to get out of my restaurant job, where absolutely none of my strengths were being used." He hit the reset button on his job search and tried a new approach that required more initiative than anything he had previously tried. This time, he started reaching out to people who worked in human resources, whether their company was hiring or not. He shared with them his interests, and how he felt he could contribute to a company. He talked about his strengths with boldness—not bragging, but not downplaying what he brought to the table either. Sometimes a contact would introduce Nick to other people in the field, and he would set more meetings. "It was a little like following a trail of breadcrumbs," Nick recalled, until one day he casually described his interests to a new contact and asked if she had any advice. The advice he received wasn't groundbreaking, but the next day, his phone vibrated with a call from that person. "Guess what, Nick?" she blurted. "I got a call today from someone looking to hire for a job that I think you'd be perfect for, given what you were telling me yesterday. I'll introduce you to her." Within the week, Nick was hired for a training and development role at a manufacturing company nearby, a job he's held ever since, and one he loves.

In all, Nick had been searching for a job for more than six months. He looks back and realizes that if he had used a better strategy earlier, he could have found something much sooner. But we don't know what we don't know. Now, Nick looks for opportunities to coach people on how to conduct a job search, based on what he learned. Nick grounded his search strategy in prayer, and as you'll read in this chapter, a lot of what ultimately helped Nick is directly supported by research on what works in the job search process. After a review of spiritual practices to support your job search, we tackle the question of what psychological science tells us regarding job search strategies that produce real results. Finally, we consider how to evaluate a job offer in light of your sense of calling.

Spiritual Practices to Sustain Your Job Search

In chapter 3, when discussing the process of discerning a calling, I outlined four spiritual practices useful for maintaining a posture of openness to God and a willingness to surrender to his will. The first of these involves setting aside time to spend in solitude and silence, closing ourselves off from clutter and distraction and creating the conditions in which our quieted hearts can surrender ourselves to God. The second involves consuming Scripture deeply, reading ourselves into the text, and prayerfully interacting with each word and phrase. The third involves prayer, which Scripture teaches us to do continually (1 Thessalonians 5:17). Discerning prayer in particular begins with an expression of quiet trust, a prayer for indifference or relinquishment of our desires in favor of God's, and a prayer for wisdom, so that we can express our freedom in making wise decisions knowing that God will use those decisions to carry out his will in our lives. Finally, the fourth spiritual practice for discernment involves self-knowledge and self-examination, looking inwardly and growing in how we understand ourselves in relation to God. These practices, when carried out in an ongoing manner, will foster an internal spiritual environment that helps you focus on God's will rather than your own. That is precisely the kind of mind-set you need to sustain your activity within a job search, in a way that keeps you focused on what is most important in your life.

You might notice that this section is short. That's because

there are no spiritual practices specifically designed to bol-
ster a job search. God is not a genie who dispenses assistance
only when we perform a certain prescribed behavior, or if we
ask for it in just the right way. There is nothing magic about
communing with God, and doing so is not merely a self-help
strategy—even though it does help. Rather, it is part of a lifestyle focused on deeply investing in your relationship with your
Creator. For that reason, the same spiritual disciplines that sustain your discernment in all of life will also sustain your focus
in your job search. Do not confuse this section's brevity with
an implication that these spiritual practices are less important
than practical, evidence-based strategies for succeeding in your
job search. Your relationship with God forms your foundation,
keeping you rooted in your desire to conform to his will in everything you do, including everything you do in your career. With
your walk with God keeping you grounded, you are free to use
the best that psychological science has to offer to inform your
job search. That's where we turn next.

What Works in a Job Search?

The number of how-to guides on conducting a job search seems
limitless, as anyone visiting the careers section of a bookstore
or Googling "job search tips" can tell you. How do you know
what actually works? A straightforward way to answer this question is to design a job search intervention containing activities
thought to work, and then to test it against a control or compar-
ison group. If the job search intervention group has better outcomes than the control group, we can conclude the intervention
is effective.

As was the case with research on career interventions
described in chapter 3, a large number of experiments testing

job search interventions have accumulated over the years. That enables researchers to conduct meta-analyses that examine the overall effects across all those studies. In one of these, Sonqi Liu, Jason L. Huang, and Mo Wang analyzed forty-seven studies with 9,575 participants.[67] The researchers were interested in answering two questions: First, do job search interventions actually help people find jobs? And second, what do the most effective interventions ask people to do?

The answer to the first question was a clear yes: job-seekers are more likely to find employment after participating in a job search intervention—around three times more likely. In exploring the second question, Liu, Huang, and Wang figured that interventions would be most effective if they operated on two levels: first, helping people improve their job search skills, and second, mobilizing their motivation to do the hard work that a job search requires. This is exactly what they found. The best job search interventions promoted skill development by helping people learn effective job search strategies and improve their self-presentation. They enhanced motivation by encouraging proactivity, promoting effective goal-setting, boosting participants' job search self-efficacy (that is, confidence in their ability to successfully carry out job search tasks), and enlisting social support. Let's address each of these in turn.

Develop Your Job Search Skills

To serve as an agent of renewal within your career path, you obviously have to secure an opportunity to work within that path. Navigating the job search process is not easy, but it starts by learning the needed skills.

1. **Effective job search strategies.** If you haven't had to carry out a formal job search before, or if it has been a long time since your last one, you may not know where to begin. The

default for many job-seekers is the same passive strategy that Nick started with: put together a résumé, search an online job board for opportunities, and then apply and wait. Some people find success this way, especially those seeking jobs in highly specialized areas with a labor shortage. Yet many people fail with this approach. Why? Part of the problem is that most job openings are never publicized and are filled via informal social networks rather than job boards.[68] Another issue is that the vast majority of job-seekers take that same passive, apply-online-and-wait approach. That means that if you rely exclusively on this approach, you're competing against the largest proportion of job-seekers for the smallest proportion of available jobs. Success is possible, but the odds are not in your favor. A better strategy is needed.

Most effective job search strategies require a much more active approach, and one that is multipronged. Let me be clear: It is perfectly fine to apply online to publicly posted positions. Doing so won't hurt you, and it is usually easy to do. In fact, PathwayU offers a job search tool with which you can enter a job title and any U.S. zip code, and publicly posted jobs will be presented for your perusal. The system even evaluates each job posting based on how well it is predicted to fit your interests and values, alerting you to jobs that are a very strong versus strong versus fair match, and so on. Browsing these listings will give you a good sense of the kinds of positions that are out there, and most postings allow you to apply directly from the site. Do not avoid online job boards in your strategy. But *do* avoid using *only* online job boards.

To understand why going beyond job boards is important, think about the hiring strategy that most employers use. Most hiring managers want to minimize risk by hiring a known quantity.[69] Ideally (for them), that means hiring someone they personally know, which is why lots of positions are filled by promoting someone from within. (This is also one of the reasons that internships have value, by the way—they often put the intern first in line for open positions.) If they can't hire from within, hiring managers typically prefer candidates who can show evidence of excellent work related to the skills required by the open position. Supplementing a résumé with an online portfolio that includes work samples is helpful in this regard. If employers can't find that, they prefer to hire someone vouched for by a trusted colleague. This highlights the value of networking—identifying people who may have connections to decision-makers at your target organization and sharing your interest in the position with them. If none of these methods work, some employers turn to recruiters to give them prescreened leads. Finally, a hiring manager who is still coming up empty will sift through the enormous pile of résumés that accumulated in response to a publicly posted job ad.

One recommended job search strategy capitalizes on the idea that the more effort people use to connect with a hiring authority they can name, regarding a position about which they have done their homework, at an organization they have come to know well, the more likely landing that job becomes. Paul Strickland, a master career counselor at the University of St. Thomas, has long urged job-seekers to count the number of active approaches they make in a given week, where *active approach* is defined as a cover letter and résumé, submitted directly to an individual in a hiring capacity, followed up with a phone call. Most job-seekers take the passive approach, starting a cover letter with "To Whom It May Concern" and ending with something like "I look forward to possibly hearing from you," thereby practically inviting a rejection. Simply making the effort to identify the hiring authority, so that you can address the letter to that person specifically, and ending with, "I will follow up with a phone call in a couple of weeks, and look forward to talking with you," can make all the difference in directing more of that person's attention to your application materials than to other job-seekers against whom you are competing. Obviously it requires effort to pursue this strategy, but that effort translates into a far greater chance of success. When Nick tried this, he began hearing back from companies, even though ultimately an even more proactive approach was needed before he secured a job offer.

Finally, as Nick learned, to access the hidden job market (those jobs that are filled without ever being publicly posted), a broader networking strategy is invaluable. Nick began conducting informational interviews (see chapters 3 and 5) to connect with people in career paths that seemed appealing to him. While interviewing them, he always made a point of sharing what kind of work seemed most engaging to him, and why. Nick scheduled these meetings to gather information, not to ask people for a job, but a positive connection eventually led someone Nick interviewed to recommend him to someone who was hiring. He worked the process, trusted it, and eventually his efforts paid off.

Beyond moving to the active end of the passive-active continuum in your job search, it also helps to realize that different types of occupations, industries, and individual companies often have their own unique and typically unwritten rules for how hiring occurs. Adapting your strategy to play by those rules, where relevant, is essential. Some industries require one-page résumés, but one-pagers look thin in other industries; a full multipage curriculum vitae instead of a résumé is expected in others. In some sectors, like some types of government work, internal hires are discouraged; positions are required to be publicly posted, and every applicant's materials must be reviewed by multiple raters on a search committee. In other sectors, especially at small, family-owned businesses, a far less formal process is used; often word-of-mouth is the only way anyone finds out about a new opportunity. Learning about these different "rules" highlights the importance of leaning on your networks. Proactively expanding those networks can help you test your assumptions and get the inside scoop. Doing this is essential, because no matter what you bring to the table as a job applicant, if you don't play by the relevant rules, you are unlikely to even be given a look.

That last paragraph comes close to framing the job search as a kind of game. I don't mean to trivialize. People's livelihoods are at stake, after all. So is your opportunity to live out your calling within a job. But in a lot of ways, viewing the process as a game is a wise strategy. Like any game, you don't win if you don't play, but you absolutely have to learn the rules and then adjust your strategy to succeed within them. Second, approaching the job search like a game has a self-protective function. No matter how well the game is played, no one wins every time. In fact, you can plan on a long string of rejections. Job expert Tom Jackson describes a typical progression of outcomes from the job search process as twenty-five "no" responses followed by a couple of yeses.[70] This is the harsh reality for most people; there is simply a lot of rejection and disappointment. The positive reframe, of course, is that every no you endure gets you one step closer to yes, and maybe to multiple yeses. Viewing the process as a game helps you see what is unfolding more objectively, and helps you view rejection as just part of the game, and nothing you should take personally.

More details on job search strategy, such as tips for effective networking, are available in the PathwayU Tools section.

2. Improve your self-presentation. Once you identify potentially good-fitting job opportunities and work to get your foot in the door, your odds for being short-listed or hired increase substantially when you present yourself well, both on paper and in an interview. Liu, Huang, and Wang found evidence that job-seekers often leave out some of the most helpful information from their résumé or organize it in a way that makes it difficult for employers to quickly identify their strengths. Instead, highlighting experiences that illustrate interpersonal skills or leadership qualities, and leading with a statement that summarizes key competencies you possess—especially those that speak to the requirements in the job ad—can significantly increase your odds of getting an interview. (Consult the PathwayU Tools section for more on preparing an effective résumé and cover letter.)

Of course, some employers no longer require a résumé, looking instead to LinkedIn, their own online application form (which typically requests the same kind of information but in a format they prefer), or even just a cover letter alone. And you can count on prospective employers Googling your name to learn more about you. According to the late career guru Dick Bolles, 91 percent of employers say they have looked up an applicant's social network profiles, and more than two-thirds have rejected applicants after seeing what was there. Keep in mind, this works the other way too—two-thirds of employers say they offered someone a job after seeing a social media profile and liking what they found. If your digital footprint reveals you to be someone who gets along well with others, communicates well, has a broad range of interests, is highly professional and highly creative, and attends well to detail (like spelling things correctly and using good grammar), you're in good shape. In contrast, if you shudder to think of what your mom might see if she Googled you, you can assume employers will feel the same way.

For better or worse, interviews are a mainstay in the hiring process.[71] Evidence suggests that job search interventions that focus on improving interview skills and reducing anxiety lead to improved interview performance and, in turn, a greater likelihood of receiving a job offer. Effective interview training often begins with very pragmatic tips on things like how to dress for an interview, the importance of making eye contact, leading with an appropriately firm handshake—all very important things to do right. Interview training also typically walks through various types of interviews you may encounter, from phone interviews to group interviews to structured and unstructured in-person interviews. You'd receive some tips for interview preparation, such as doing your homework on the opportunity and the organization and having responses ready for commonly asked questions. Savvy interviewees also are prepared to use the STAR technique, in which (whether directly prompted or not) they share stories that describe a Situation, Task, Action, and Result from their education or work history to highlight their strengths and illustrate how they will perform on the job. For example, imagine you are interviewing for a customer service position. Somewhere in the interview, you might tell a story about a time you were charged with the unpleasant task of appeasing an angry customer (situation), how you listened attentively to ensure that the customer felt heard and understood before consulting with a sympathetic supervisor (task), and how you then offered a reasonable solution to the concerns (action), with the outcome of de-escalating the situation and helping the customer feel valued, even if still somewhat upset (result). These kinds of interview tips and others are available in the PathwayU Tools section. Reviewing those, and arranging opportunities to practice your skills, will improve your performance.

When discussing self-presentation, it goes without saying

(although I'll say it anyway) that you have to approach the process with authenticity and integrity. Tailoring résumés, cover letters, and interviews to emphasize your fit to a position is part of playing the game, but it is absolutely essential to be completely truthful in what you are conveying to employers, whether on paper, online, or in an interview. Truth-telling is a moral duty in a job search. Furthermore, the consequences for fabrication and embellishment are severe, as Scott Thompson (CEO of Yahoo), Sandra Baldwin (president of the U.S. Olympic Committee), Kenneth Lonchar (CFO of Veritas Software Corp.), and George O'Leary (football coach at Notre Dame) discovered. All four were fired from their lofty positions and publicly humiliated after people discovered falsified information on their résumés.

Finally, effective self-presentation requires humility. Humility is a virtue—one embodied in the person of Jesus Christ—that includes an accurate evaluation of the self (not thinking too much or too little of oneself), and a focus on others' welfare at least as much as one's own. I mention this virtue in part to stress that humility is not the same thing as modesty, which involves being self-effacing and unpretentious, often to a fault. In a job search, modestly downplaying your strengths will not do you any favors, but humility exudes a quiet confidence that can endear you to employers without compromising your integrity. Nick grappled with the difference between modesty and humility in his job search. "Both of my parents exemplify modesty," he expressed. "Especially my dad, who never wanted to imply in any way that he was better than someone else. He wanted everyone to judge him purely on his actions, which he said were louder than words. I respect that approach and I internalized it. Also, I personally can't stand when people are arrogant. But I overcompensated—and constantly downplayed my strengths and skills."

In his current role in human resources, Nick often assists in the hiring process for his company. "It's really interesting seeing it from the other side. I can see now that by never naming my strengths, I wasn't differentiating myself from anyone, and my job search was going nowhere. When I interview people like that now, they come across as not only very average candidates, but they almost seem disinterested in the position. I was doing this same thing when I was looking for a job. At some point I realized that I wasn't even being honest with employers about the skills I brought to the table."

Nick noticed that people in his life were picking up on this. "I would get feedback from my friends telling me that when I started to talk about myself, I'd always leave out the things that were most descriptive and impressive," he recalled.

> No wonder my job search was such a battle! Eventually I realized that I needed to talk about the gifts that I have—not to brag about anything, but to offer examples to assure them that I would excel in this role. In the position I'm in now, they wanted someone who in part could influence the culture here in a positive way, through building healthy, positive relationships at work. I am really good at that; it's right in my wheelhouse, and I gained enough confidence to say as much. Doing so made all the difference. I told the truth about myself, and I got the job.

One could argue that it is an affront to your Creator, whose image you bear, to leave out or downplay during your job search process the assets that will help you thrive in the job. Self-promotion with humility means not overselling, but not underselling either. Express your strengths confidently and with authenticity. "You are a child of God, and you were born to manifest the glory of God," Nick recalled. "I repeated that to keep myself from downplaying my strengths in this process. It became my mantra." Let it be yours too.

Keep the Pedal Down (That Is, Stay Motivated)

The most effective job search interventions recognize that once you've learned and practiced key job search skills, deploying them with persistence requires motivation, especially when rejections pile up and the process takes longer than you ever would have expected. Liu, Huang, and Wang found that the most successful job search interventions foster motivation using four critical ingredients, which I review next.

3. **Stay proactive.** Job-seekers often drift into passivity in the job search, gradually adapting to the status quo rather than taking the initiative needed to speed up a successful outcome. It is easy to feel motivated when first embarking on a job search, but when days become weeks, and especially if weeks become months, that motivation becomes very hard to sustain. Interventions that succeed in reversing this drift into passivity instead encourage proactivity and do so in several ways. One is to urge job-seekers to expand the range of positions they are targeting to include some that exceed their qualifications. Job-seekers are often surprised by this, but many employers provide on-the-job training and are happy to hire candidates who meet the minimum qualifications, if their interests, values, and personality fit the position well. "Hire for fit, train for talent" is the axiom that describes this approach. Adding this to your strategy increases the volume of positions you can go after; that's where the need for more proactivity arises.

Another way of encouraging greater proactivity is to adopt Strickland's "active approach," mentioned earlier, by calling a hiring manager after sending a résumé. Doing that is not easy; it requires some investigation to identify the person doing the hiring—and some gumption to call. A third way is to expand your networking strategy using the informational interview approach that Nick used. Still other ways of expressing proactivity include taking the initiative to provide employers with additional job-related information not requested (perhaps a written case study describing a past success that is relevant for that job), asking former employers for recommendation letters and personal referrals, and even asking employers who do not have any job openings to recommend other employers who they know are hiring. All of these are examples of "above and beyond" job search behaviors that combat passivity and increase the odds of landing a job, and landing one faster.

4. **Set smarter goals.** Recall that written goal setting was one of the critical ingredients in effective career decision-making interventions, just as it is in effective job search interventions. Job search behaviors are easy to connect with clearly stated goals that meet the conditions of smarter goals I reviewed in chapter 3, and evidence suggests that clearly stated job search goals are positively linked to job search intensity, which is in turn related to job search success.[72] To harness the impact of smarter goals, some of the especially effective interventions identified in Liu, Huang, and Wang's meta-analysis required weekly meetings with a counselor to review progress toward reaching one's current goals, and also setting new goals for the next meeting. If you are working with a counselor, this is a useful way of structuring your time together. If you are not, try building in this type of accountability using one or more of the members of your Personal Board of Advisers, whom you named in chapter 3. Goal-setting is critical in helping job-seekers stay proactive, sustaining their attention and effort.

5. **Boost your job search self-efficacy.** *Self-efficacy* refers to people's beliefs that they can successfully carry out a particular task.[73] This is different from self-esteem, which is global in nature; self-efficacy always pertains to a specific task. I might have high self-esteem—a positive view of myself in general— while simultaneously having low self-efficacy for carrying out various elements of a job search. Similarly, one might have high self-efficacy for some tasks (like submitting an application online) and low self-efficacy for others (like networking). Research on job search self-efficacy is very clear: self-efficacy is strongly associated with effective job search behaviors, the number of job offers received, and employment status.[74]

Why does self-efficacy make such a big difference? There are a few reasons. First, people who believe they are highly capable of doing something set higher goals. Job-seekers with high self-efficacy set their sights on completing more job applications each week, contacting more employers, and securing more interviews compared to those with low self-efficacy for those tasks. Second, when people have high self-efficacy for a particular task—say, cold-calling hiring managers—they tend to show higher levels of commitment toward that task and greater interest in engaging in it. You can see how self-efficacy ties to motivation in this way; we want to engage in activities we feel confident we can do well. In fact, we feel satisfied when we've mastered a challenge, and anticipating that sense of satisfaction gives us motivation to persist in it. Push yourself to see those cold calls as a challenge that you can master. Third, when people have high self-efficacy for a task and they experience failure, they tend to attribute the failure to a lack of effort, whereas people with low self-efficacy assume that failure is due to a lack of ability. Certainly, "I just don't have what it takes to do this well" kills a person's motivation, whereas "I could do this better if I tried harder" has the opposite effect. In short, increasing your self-efficacy can sustain you, even when you face challenges and setbacks in the job search. When applying this to your own life, the key questions are: How confident are you in your ability to carry out your search successfully, and how can you become more confident? The stronger your self-efficacy for your job search, the better your outcomes are likely to be.

You can boost your self-efficacy by paying attention to four sources of self-efficacy beliefs: your past performance, your ability to learn by observing others, authentic encouragement you receive from people, and your internal emotional state. Effective job search interventions target these sources to increase self-efficacy. One study tested an intervention that used video clips depicting people carrying out specific job search behaviors well, followed by discussion and a chance to role-play that behavior in small groups, where participants can get feedback and encouragement.[75] Watching someone model the behavior, then practicing it and receiving encouragement and feedback, targets three of the four sources of self-efficacy beliefs—and evidence from that study revealed that more frequent and successful job search behavior in the "real world" was the result. Add to that a meditative prayer to seek God's help in quelling the anxiety that wells up within you while you anticipate a job search task, and all four sources are addressed. To summarize, learning from people who have successfully navigated a job search, trying out the skills yourself, leaning on encouragement from people in your life, and prayerfully calming your anxiety will boost your self-efficacy and lead to positive results.

6. Enlist support. The final critical ingredient in effective job search interventions involves enlisting social support. Numerous studies have found that social support is associated with how much effort job-seekers expend in their job search. One

study found that support from a spouse predicted positive attitudes and expectations on the part of the job-seeker.[76] Another
found that the level of support from family and friends predicted the intensity of a job-seeker's search.[77] In response to
this evidence, job search interventions now routinely involve
family, friends, and other people in job-seekers' lives who can
provide support—both emotional support like encouragement
and assurance and tangible support such as help with trans-
portation or child care. Interventions also urge job seekers seek
help with things like reviewing a cover letter or resume, practicing an interview, or identifying new job leads. Group coun
seling interventions make heavy use of peer support, mutual
encouragement, trading résumé feedback, and sharing job
leads. Interventions that use these kinds of techniques to enlist
social support produce better outcomes than interventions that
disregard the social aspects of the process.

Recall that social support was also a critical ingredient identified by Brown and Ryan Krane in their meta-analysis of career
decision-making interventions. Indeed, social support has been
found in research to provide countless benefits across a wide
range of challenges.[78] This consistent finding speaks to the fundamental importance of not going it alone but walking alongside others who can support you as you face your challenges.
Human beings are created to be in community, both to serve
and to be served. This is the biblical model, evident starting in
early Genesis (2:18) and a consistent theme throughout Scripture. The power of social support also happens to be thoroughly
supported by psychological research. Don't hesitate to lean into
it. Navigating your job search by yourself is a recipe for frustration, failure, and pain. More than that, doing so denies those
who love you a chance to express the care they have for you.
Others will need you when they face challenging tasks they must

carry out in their lives, and you will have opportunities to support them. But when you are the one navigating a difficult transition—such as a job search—seek the support you need. Doing so is life-giving for everyone involved.

Evaluate Job Offers in Light of Your Calling

As you use the job search skills you learn, and persist in implementing them even in the face of frustration, you will eventually receive job offers.[79] How should you evaluate those offers as they come in, given your sense of calling? Granted, it is a luxury to have choice in the matter, a luxury you may not possess right now. Your circumstances may be such that you simply must accept whatever offer you can secure. Maybe you have only one job offer to evaluate, and it is hard to see that others will follow quickly. Maybe you are reading this in a geographic region or at a time in which jobs in your field are hard to find. Even so, whether you have one or several job offers, the key issue is what you can expect from this job, in terms of how it fits with your calling. The following questions can help you assess your possibilities.

Does This Position Align with Your Gifts?

This was a central question in chapters 4 and 5, except there you were evaluating career paths or occupations more broadly. When you receive an offer for a job, you must now evaluate fit on a more specific level. Think back on your interests, values, personality, and abilities. Read the job description carefully and imagine yourself in that role, day in and day out. If you are still unsure of how that will look, ask if you can speak to some of your prospective coworkers to get a clearer sense of their experience. Investigate questions such as:

- Will the essential requirements of the job capture what you most enjoy?
- Will it satisfy your strongest work values?
- Will it allow you to "be who you are," like a swimmer paddling with the current rather than fighting against it?
- Do the abilities required for the job overlap well with your strengths?

Remember, behind these questions is the biblical vision of people with different gifts, each finding opportunities to express those gifts, for God's glory and the common good. Remember also that a key way to discern your calling is to identify your gifts and explore opportunities that fit them. If this job will allow you to express your gifts, chances are good it falls within the range of opportunities that align with your calling.

Can You Thrive in This Organization's Culture?

This question moves from evaluating the essential duties of the job to examining the culture of the organization. The question is one of workplace culture preferences: does this employer embrace the organizational values most important to you? Organizations vary widely in the types of cultures that they promote. For example, some emphasize innovation and give employees every opportunity to tinker and transform; others take an "if it ain't broke, don't fix it" approach and stress the importance of consistency and quality. Some are mission-driven, socially responsible, and self-reflective; others are laser-focused on their goals for performance. As was the case for interests, values, and personality, PathwayU measures your workplace preferences to help you gain a sense of what will be most important for you to experience from an organization.

Attempts to measure differences in workplace preferences—

both in the cultural values that people prefer, and in the cultural values that organizations promote—date to a series of studies at Berkeley during the early 1990s. There, researchers generated a set of fifty-four value statements that could be used to describe any person or organization, but that couldn't be used to describe *all* people or organizations—terms like "rule-oriented," "precise," and "socially responsible." Researchers put those statements on a set of cards and asked a group of people to sort those cards into piles based on how descriptive each statement was of their *current* organization and their *ideal* organization. That process was repeated and refined several times, and each time, a series of sophisticated statistical analyses were applied to the ratings. A decade ago, scholars from Australia reduced the items further, and researchers at jobZology continued refining the instrument until arriving at seven broad dimensions of workplace culture. They are as follows:

- *Excellence*. People who value excellence like working for organizations that emphasize achievement, quality, being distinctive from others, and being competitive.
- *Guiding principles*. People who value guiding principles like working for organizations that value social responsibility, have a clear guiding philosophy, are reflective in their approach to doing business, and have a good reputation.
- *Collaboration*. People who value collaboration like working for organizations that are team- or people-oriented, share information freely, and emphasize working together to reach shared goals.
- *Innovation*. People who value innovation like working for organizations that are quick to take advantage of

opportunities, emphasize creativity, are comfortable taking risks, and encourage employees to take individual responsibility.

- *Recognition.* People who value recognition like working for organizations that place a strong emphasis on fairness, provide praise and high pay for good performance, and offer opportunities for professional growth.
- *Performance.* People who value performance like working for organizations that have high expectations, are results-oriented and highly organized, and have high levels of enthusiasm for the job.
- *Stability.* People who value stability like working for organizations where the level of conflict is low, where job security is high, and where people are calm.

Which of these workplace culture values would your ideal organization emphasize? As was the case for the work values discussed in chapter 4, PathwayU uses a forced-choice format to measure workplace preferences, requiring you to prioritize which organizational values are most important for you. When you do so, which ones rise to the top? Understanding your preferences can help you evaluate a prospective employer based on the fit of its values with yours. For me, guiding principles are of primary importance, and recognition is my second highest score. My university and the company I cofounded both are mission-driven organizations, which makes their cultures an excellent fit for my preference for guiding principles. In terms of recognition, high performance is not always recognized in the ways I'd prefer, but opportunities for professional development abound. To get a feel for an organization's culture, you can examine its website and talk with people who are familiar with the organization. Those are great starting points, but make sure you also talk with current employees, especially the folks who would be your coworkers and team members.

Can You Live Your Calling within the Job?

One recurring point in this book is that, for most of us, our callings transcend any particular job title; a job is simply a vehicle through which we can express our gifts to glorify God and serve the common good. In the ideal world, you will receive an offer for a job that aligns well with your gifts at an organization with a culture that supports what is most important to you—a position tailor-made for you that will align perfectly with your calling. But for better or worse, all of us live in the real world, not the ideal world. In the real world, some level of compromise is, as far as I can tell, universal; each of us can expect to work in a role in which the fit is less than perfect. When you are evaluating job offers, imagine a continuum along which you can place jobs based on how well each fits your calling, from perfect alignment to no alignment at all. For any job, ask yourself: Where along that continuum does this job fall? How well will this job allow me to use my gifts to glorify God by cultivating God's creation in redemptive ways that enhance the common good? Let your answers to these questions drive your decisions.

Whether you have lots of choice in the matter or very little, accepting a job offer is not the end of the discernment process. Landing a job simply moves new questions to the forefront: How can you move your career forward in a way that prepares you for the inevitable future changes? How can you work in a way that roots your story in Scripture's Four-Act Story? These questions are the focus of the final section of the book.

PART 3

Living Your Calling

CHAPTER 7

Living a Calling in a Changing World of Work

THERE WAS a time when people looking for work in countries like the United States could reasonably expect to find a job close to home and stay employed within a single organization for a long time. That employer would define its employees' career paths over the next few decades, then gift them a gold watch and pay a pension when they retired. An implicit sweat-for-security agreement formed the basis of this arrangement, with the employee promising a consistent effort in exchange for a stable job and a well-defined corporate ladder to climb. Such jobs still exist, of course, but they are now the exception rather than the rule. A new kind of labor agreement has emerged, one in which people find themselves trading security for flexibility.

Around the same time the sweat-for-security agreement was commonplace, people also expected a familiar rhythm to their work. Most professionals could expect a short drive to an office where they would interact face-to-face every day with supervisors and coworkers. Most everyone could plan to clock in at 9 a.m. and clock out at 5 p.m. (more or less), allowing them to "leave work at work" when they returned home. Today, empowered by (mostly) seamless videoconferencing technology and ubiquitous online availability, an increasing number of workers enjoy flexible schedules and work remotely. They work more hours than people did in the past, but they have more control over their schedules—although maybe not so much when conferencing in to a meeting at 2 a.m. with a team located on the other side of the globe. Major shifts in the way people communicate, shop, build relationships, and consume content have created major disruptions in the types of jobs that people believe are needed, as well as in the types of jobs that are *actually* needed. More tech jobs are available, sure. But the reality is that most every job is becoming a tech job, and every company is becoming a tech company.

The increasing influence of tech obviously has a tremendous upside, with innovative new conveniences and efficiencies. Automation and artificial intelligence give us digital administrative assistants to coordinate our schedules, digital accountants to balance our books, and soon, self-driving vehicles to deliver our goods and get us where we need to go. These are wins—unless you're the human administrative assistant, accountant, or driver being displaced. As robots become increasingly sophisticated, anxiety builds, and more and more people wonder how long it will take before they are displaced too. To fan the flame, news outlets warn of a shockingly near future in which huge swaths of the workforce are replaced by machines, ultimately leading to a world in which little human work will be needed at all.[80]

For better or worse, one major consequence of the accumulating change in today's work world is that people bear more responsibility than ever for managing their own careers. In some ways, this reality might be paralyzing; it puts a lot of pressure on you, because you cannot rely on an employer to chart out a path for you to follow. But it also represents an important opportunity. In pursuing your calling, you have the freedom to lean on your identity in Christ while updating your skills and learning new, innovative ways to adapt to the changing work world. In doing so, you will learn ways to create opportunities that better align your gifts with needs in the world, for God's glory. In this chapter we lay out in some detail the new normals[81] in today's world of work, then explore how Christians might respond effectively.

New Normal #1:
We've Traded Security for Flexibility

Collectively, workers are giving up security for greater flexibility in proportions that are increasing by the day. "Flexibility" here means that people have more options than ever regarding when, where, and for whom their work is performed. This stems from a dramatic rise in contingent work arrangements in which companies hire contractors for short-term projects rather than loyal employees to whom they commit for the long haul. For companies, hiring only when they need help and cutting someone loose when a project ends is appealing because costs stay low. In response to this trend, more and more workers have embraced self-employment, signing up for two- to four-year "tours of duty" with employers, organized around specific projects.[82] Many people cobble together multiple ways to make a living, working as independent contractors, consultants, or freelancers. In fact, freelance work was projected to occupy 43 percent of the U.S. economy in 2020, up from 35 percent in 2017.[83] But, while the gig economy offers people freedom and variety, it also leaves them vulnerable, with few benefits or perks (forget about healthcare or paid vacation time) and little if any loyalty on the part of organizations (which, for their part, are also scrambling to find new ways to succeed). Remember Jayla from chapters 4 and 5? She loved her work as a maker with a custom jewelry business, but it proved too hard for her to sustain a living on that gig alone. With more and more full-time jobs giving way to project-based contracts, the crazy pace of job transitions will only increase.

Frequent job change, already the name of the game for most workers, will likely shape your experience throughout the course of your career.

New Normal #2:
Every Company Is a Tech Company

Technology is rapidly becoming a fundamental part of virtually all jobs, not just the ones located in Silicon Valley. Signs of this transition are everywhere. Where there once were clipboards, now there are iPads. Paper billing feels inefficient and quaint; it can all be handled through an app. Brick-and-mortar retail stores and suburban shopping malls are falling further and further behind online retailers whose wares are available to buy anytime, in the palm of your hand. We've moved way past mainframes, end-user computing, and the novelty of a connected global network. Today, computing technology permeates almost everything, giving people unlimited electronic access to virtually anything they need, anytime from anywhere. The line between the physical and digital worlds is now so blurred that it barely exists. According to organizational psychologists Wayne Cascio and Ramiro Montealegre, developers pushing those technologies are striving for "an optimized space that links people, computers, networks, and objects, thereby overcoming the limitations of both the physical world and the electronic space."[84] How does this impact how you experience your work? Here are some examples:

- If monitoring is part of your job, such as keeping track of temperature, humidity, light, sound, and even the locking of doors and the opening and closing of windows, this can all be handled remotely now.

- If you handle inventory, this can now be automatically monitored and refreshed on a rolling basis, introducing customers to additional items and services in real time.
- If your job involves driving, traffic data is increasingly used to set delivery routes and schedules, and your employer may be tracking your location, engine status, road conditions, and safe driving behavior in real time.
- Education and training are now available anytime thanks to online tutorials, whether through paid platforms like Lynda or free platforms like YouTube.
- Wearable technology embedded with chips and sensors (on wrists, on glasses, in clothing, and even implanted under the skin[85]) is now part of a growing number of workplaces. This technology gathers information about stress levels, injuries, and other indicators of physical state and health status for purposes of effort monitoring, assisting in emergency situations, or facilitating preventative treatment.

These are just some of the ways that ubiquitous computing is changing how work is carried out. Whatever your profession, the ability to adapt to new and emerging technologies is increasingly a fundamental requirement for success —not just in tech jobs, but in any job.

New Normal #3:
The Robots Are Coming

An HBO *VICE Special Reports* episode titled "The Future of Work"[86] opened with an autonomous truck navigating portions of I-10 near Tucson. Picture an eighteen-wheeler outfitted with sensors, cameras, lasers, and a head-spinning amount of computing power, but otherwise identical to the semis you pass each time you drive on the freeway. Because the technology is still in a testing phase, a human sat in the driver's seat, but that person quickly proved superfluous as the truck traveled its route flawlessly. This wonder of technology is the creation of TuSimple, one of several companies hoping to increase safety, cut costs, and reduce carbon emissions using fleets of self-driving trucks. The stakes are high. Trucking is the most common occupation among American men, and in total, there are 3.5 million truck drivers in the United States alone. When truck-stop restaurants, convenience stores, service stations, and other services connected to the industry are accounted for, nearly 8 million jobs hang in the balance.[87]

It's worth the reminder that these statistics represent real people. Recognizing this, "The Future of Work" introduced viewers to Don, a tattooed, bearded owner-operator of a trucking company. When asked what he loves about his job, Don beamed. "Oh gosh," he said. "I love to drive! For me, it's a privilege. It's a privilege to get out there, get behind the wheel of eighty thousand pounds, drive that thing down the road. . . . And I know I'm providing the U.S.—I'm providing the world—with whatever I got in the back of my freight. I deliver your clothes, your food that you're eating. A lot of people don't see that! And it's a good feeling as a driver, as a human being." His voice was steady and assured, and his passion and sense of purpose were undeniable, even inspiring. But after Don was introduced to the featured autonomous truck, his voice fell: "What would I do if I didn't drive? I can't honestly answer that 'cause I really don't know what I would do. I'd . . . I'd be scared."

Trucking is just one industry among many for which automation and artificial intelligence poses both a major opportunity and a major threat. Robots have worked in factories for decades, but the early robots were mostly enormous, expensive machines that performed only a single task, like riveting or welding. Today's robots are a different story. They are far cheaper, smaller, and safer. They also are increasingly capable of making complex judgments, even learning to carry out new tasks on their own, in uncertain and changing situations. As a result, the types of jobs supposedly at risk of becoming obsolete due to automation are broadening in scope. An oft-cited Oxford University study estimated that 47 percent of U.S. jobs could be automated within the next decade or two.[88] The story is far worse for other countries; the same Oxford research group more recently predicted that with drones, wearable sensors, self-help kiosks, speech recognition, eye-tracking technology, 3D printers, and self-learning software, 69 percent of jobs in India and 77 percent in China are at risk of replacement.[89] There are already examples of what this might look like. For example, one eighty-six-thousand-square-foot factory in Japan (which, ironically, makes industrial robots) is staffed by just four people.[90] The threat of automation is not solely a problem for blue-collar workers, either. Staffing for corporate finance departments shrank by 40 percent between 2004 and 2015 as accounting tasks became progressively automated with robust software. In the past, it was blacksmiths and lamplighters, then elevator operators and telephone switchboard workers, then video store owners whose jobs became almost completely obsolete. Today, along with truck drivers, it is the likes of accounts receivable clerks, bookkeepers, and inventory control workers whose days on the job seem numbered.

More Than Survival

The massive changes described above point to some unsettling uncertainties. Of course, concern about drastic work changes due to technological development is nothing new. A little more than two hundred years ago, a group of textile workers in England—artisans who had spent years developing their skills—were confronted with automated looms and knitting frames that mechanized the task of weaving. With their entire way of life about to unravel, the most desperate of these weavers grabbed sledgehammers and began smashing the machines and setting fire to factories. They hoped their efforts would prompt the government to ban weaving machines, but instead, machine-breaking was outlawed and made punishable by death, effectively crushing their rebellion. These workers were known as the Luddites, a term now synonymous with "technophobe."[91]

Fighting against the tide of change in today's world of work would prove as fruitless for us as it did for the Luddites in the early nineteenth century. A more effective strategy is to adapt—and not only to adapt, but to shape the direction of these new normals in life-giving ways. But how? Vocational psychologists point to two approaches Christians can take to successfully navigate the changing world of work: career adaptability and planned happenstance. Undergirding these strategies, God's grand story points to our need to affirm our calling as God's image-bearers, recognize Christ's lordship over all of creation, and engage the changing world of work redemptively.

Build Career Adaptability

A key path toward thriving in the changing world of work is to develop *career adaptability*, which refers to your readiness and resources for coping with "tasks, transitions, and traumas"[92] in your career. Some transitions people face are expected, like finding employment after finishing a degree. Others, like getting laid off (remember Alejandro in chapter 3?), may feel like they come out of nowhere. Nearly all transitions, whether good or bad, are stressful, requiring adaptability to manage successfully. Across ninety studies, research reveals that people's career adaptability is linked to numerous beneficial outcomes, including a strong career identity, a sense of calling, reduced job stress, enhanced employability and promotability, and increased engagement, job performance, job and life satisfaction, and positive emotions.[93] Adapting within one's career journey, in other words, bears fruit.[94]

Four types of psychological resources assist in building career adaptability: concern, control, curiosity, and confidence. The most important aspect of career adaptability is *concern*, or the motivation to prepare for future possibilities. Career concern flows out of a future orientation—a sense that to be successful in the future, it helps to prepare now. Concern includes an optimistic attitude of planfulness, one that drives you to learn more about what you'll likely face both in the near term and the distant future. Career concern is fostered by looking back and realizing that where you are now is a product of your past experiences—experiences you can build on to prepare you for a future where you can express your gifts in new ways. In a world of work defined by constant change, anticipating that change and developing an attitude of preparedness will position you well to manage it when it arrives.

A second component of adaptability is *control* over your future career. Control in this sense means self-discipline—that is, taking an organized, deliberate, decisive approach to making choices and managing transitions. Having control means recognizing you are not merely a passive recipient of external forces in the world of work, but rather you are an active shaper of your career trajectory. Career control does *not* mean ignoring the promptings of the Holy Spirit or failing to surrender to God. The opposite of this type of control is not surrender, but rather confusion, impulsivity, or avoidance. You can and should maintain an attitude of surrender to God's providence while still actively managing your career, accepting personal responsibility, and making career decisions with wisdom. One of the paradoxical advantages of the new trading-security-for-flexibility labor contract is that you can no longer rely on a stable employer to map out your career path. Instead, you are in the driver's seat of your own career development. You have the latitude to make your own decisions, aware of your dependence and reliance on God for strength and wisdom in living your calling.

A third dimension of career adaptability, *curiosity*, emerges from a sense of control. Curiosity involves taking the initiative to figure out new ways to translate your skills into opportunities. It requires inquisitiveness—an eagerness to explore—and transforms a person from naïve to knowledgeable. Curiosity builds on a willingness to mentally project oneself into new roles, imagining what they would be like and identifying what is needed for success. Doing this, over time, fosters new skills, greater self-awareness, and a clearer understanding of new ways to work. The broader the array of information that results from your curiosity, the more informed your choices can be. Beware of narrow job training programs that focus solely on skills that will prove obsolete in a decade while overlooking a broader approach to ongoing skill development. Job skills are critical, but even more critical is "learning how to learn" so that you can adapt as needs in the world change and as new technologies are introduced. Leaning into your curiosity will spur on personal growth, promote your ability to roll with change, and help you thoughtfully harness new technologies and new ways of working as you live out your calling.

Finally, career adaptability requires *confidence*. People have confidence when they look ahead and see themselves encountering but overcoming barriers in their career. Confidence means feeling assured you will do what it takes to live out your calling in the world of work, despite knowing it won't always be easy. Some of the barriers you may confront are internal, like self-doubt. Others are external, like those rooted in inequities based on social class, gender, or race, which limit access to valuable opportunities. These barriers are enormously challenging, but confidence grows when you believe they are surmountable.[95] A lack of confidence leaves a person unwilling to take risks, preferring to avoid failure by not trying. That strategy offers short-term anxiety relief but thwarts progress toward longer-term goals. Christians possess an existential confidence from knowing we are held by God in love (Romans 8:38–39), but this doesn't always translate into career confidence. Presenting your career concerns to God in prayer (Philippians 4:6–7) while engaging in active problem-solving and leaning on your support system will help you grow the confidence you need.

Use Planned Happenstance; Experience God's Providence

Having a planful approach for the future is important, but how do you pair this with the reality that most people, when asked how they arrived at where they are today, attribute at least some of their position to events that seem completely outside their control? Unexpected twists and turns are common. One study found nearly two-thirds of older adults identified a serendipitous, seemingly random event that influenced their career trajectory in a nontrivial way.[96]

Vocational psychologists have studied these supposedly random events and tend to view them as not random at all. Instead, they call this phenomenon *planned happenstance.* Planned happenstance starts with the idea that it's important to live an active life—trying new things, introducing yourself to new people, learning about them, listening to them, and sharing your plans and passions with them. The more you do these kinds of things, the more likely it becomes that one of these interactions will introduce a legitimate opportunity that opens new pathways for living your calling. The key in leveraging planned happenstance is not merely to identify, evaluate, and pursue unexpected opportunities when they come up, although doing so is important. Rather, the key is to *create* those opportunities. The more actively you engage life, the more of these opportunities you will encounter. The point is to live boldly, with vigor and without fear, constantly trying new things and putting yourself out there. Do these things, and then expect the unexpected.

What does it look like, practically, to live out a calling using career adaptability and planned happenstance? Consider Alissa. She is a professor at King's College in New York City, teaching writing, criticism, and cultural theory. She also serves as a staff writer for Vox. Before Vox, she was chief film critic at *Christianity Today* and spent a decade writing on pop culture and art for outlets like *Rolling Stone* and *The Atlantic*. She is regarded as "one of the most prolific, eloquent, and creative culture critics working today."[97] How did she get there?

"I don't think I ever really did make a conscious choice," she told *FORMA*:[98]

> It was just a natural extension of my everyday life to pitch reviews to editors for movies I was going to see anyway. . . . I was good enough at writing that people kept asking me to do it, and if you stick around long enough and have a knack for it, the work starts to snowball. But there was no moment where I sat down and said, "I would like to become a critic, and here

are the steps I will follow to do that." I know people who have done that, but it wouldn't have worked for me. I didn't set out to become a teacher. But like most people with a master's degree, I needed to earn a little money on the side and started adjuncting,[99] teaching first-year English composition classes. That turned into a full faculty position teaching the same subject for a few years. But I'd landed at a college that was growing its program in media, culture, and the arts, and when they asked me to teach courses on cultural theory and criticism as well, I could hardly refuse.

In general, though, for the first seven or eight years of my career, I just pitched articles haphazardly as they occurred to me, and whenever someone offered me work doing something—whether or not I thought I was fully qualified for it at the time—I said yes, and figured out how to do it afterwards. That's led to criticism and teaching. But it wasn't a path I set out on, nor do I really think I would have thought of it as a career path until recently.

Alissa describes her career as more of a gradual unfolding than the result of careful planning. Career experts would urge a more goal-oriented strategy, yet Alissa's experience nevertheless reveals a process of ongoing adaptation. While growing up, she read books incessantly and was a classically trained pianist by the time she entered adulthood. Both of these helped prepare her for concentrating deeply on art for long periods of time. But pitching editors, writing engaging reviews, and developing effective learning experiences for students—these were skills Alissa developed in response to opportunities she saw in front of her and opportunities she created. All of these tasks align with the interests and abilities God created her with, and all of them support her mission of engaging in the work of translation—that is, "figuring out how to express things in terms that people who might not think those things are 'for them' can understand," as she described to me.

In your own career path, cultivate your ability to adapt to a constantly changing world of work. Use planned happenstance to create new opportunities. When a promising opportunity emerges, even one you might never have imagined, evaluate how well it fits who you are—your interests, values, personality, abilities, and workplace preferences. Ask yourself:

- Is the fit there?
- Do my current circumstances allow for it?
- Have I discussed the possibility with important people in my life, like my Personal Board of Advisers?
- Have I prayed over the matter?
- Can I envision expressing my gifts through this path in ways that are redemptive?

If your answer to questions like these is yes, then jump on the opportunity with confidence. I think career adaptability and planned happenstance, when layered onto a view of God as sovereign and fully in control of your destiny, are incredibly exciting.

Embrace Your Image-Bearer Identity

World-of-work changes like those reviewed in this chapter are exciting for some workers but evoke fear for many others. For some, such changes call into question our ingrained assumption that if we are reasonably capable and work hard, we'll be rewarded with a vibrant career. What if that is not the case? If we can't count on a stable work future, what do we do? Econo-mists Kevin Brown and Steven McMullen suggest the anxiety we experience in response to this question reflects a culturally influenced "materialist narrative." According to the material-ist narrative, we are all simply trying to survive, and our worth is determined by our hard work and the rewards we reap (e.g., money, privilege, and power) from the market.[100] This bleak view defines our personal value by our economic value. If this materialist narrative reflects reality, we are right to be anxious about disloyal employers, rampant job change, technological transformation, and eager robots on hand to replace us. Any of these things can rob us of our value, and their combination may strip us of it entirely.

However, Brown and McMullen also point out what the mate-rialist narrative misses. All of us want to survive, sure, but our value is not defined by what we produce or consume. We are relational beings with moral compasses. We strive to meet our own needs, but we also care about others. We express empa-thy and show compassion. We build communities. We also create, design, invent, produce, transform. This is a different narrative—an image-bearing narrative that reminds us of our place within God's grand story. In this narrative, our value is defined by the fact that God loves us, created us in his image (Genesis 1:26–27), and sent his Son to give us new life (John 3:16). Remember the big picture of God's Four-Act Story: God created all things and declared them good. All things became tainted and distorted by sin. All things are redeemed by Jesus's work on the cross. And all things will one day be made new, when Christ returns to usher in the new heavens and the new earth. As God's image-bearer, you are charged with the task of developing God's creation and partnering in his work of redemption.

Accepting responsibility for this role in God's story gives us resources for managing the changing world of work with confidence rather than anxiety. As God's image-bearer, you can rest assured that your callings within your various life roles, including your work, are ultimately not threatened by robots, artificial intelligence, or any other entity that does not bear God's image. To say this does not deny the real challenges we face in our current world of work. As was the case for the Luddites, workers in some types of jobs today—especially low-skilled jobs in manufacturing, food service, and construction[101]—are undeniably vulnerable to displacement due to automation. For these workers especially, accessing education, developing new skills, and increasing career adaptability are essential. Ensuring that they receive the support they need represents a critical responsibility for society, one the church can help to address.[102]

Still, there is reason for optimism. New technologies have a long track record of disrupting economies by shifting where work is needed and requiring updated sets of skills, but ordinarily they create more jobs than they eliminate. In fact, in all of history, new technologies have *never* resulted in a net decrease in the number of available jobs.[103] This reality offers one reason to take a breath. But from an image-bearing perspective, there is still more cause for optimism. All legitimate work is a form of service, but not all work is equally meaningful. So when mind-numbingly repetitive tasks are automated, workers have more opportunity for creativity, collaboration, and service. In other words, they can more readily express the positive aspects of being uniquely human, created in God's image for his glory. "Technological disruption is not simply displacement from work," according to Brown and McMullen, "but also can be an invitation to other forms of work that may allow us to better exercise an array of God-reflecting capacities."[104]

Christians within workplaces of all kinds are best-positioned to promote an image-bearing narrative in the face of existential threats in today's world of work. Treating coworkers and customers fairly is an obvious step, but an image-bearing focus also includes investing in ongoing skill development. Continuous retraining can help ensure that new technologies result in enhanced skills rather than an endangered livelihood. Expressing your own gifts for creative and redemptive service while encouraging others to do the same, for the well-being of the whole, aligns with the biblical vision of life in community. In a time of looming career disruption, you can help lead the way in shaping a new, redemptive narrative for work, one in which people embrace their image-bearing identity to "seek first God's kingdom and his righteousness," resting assured that "all these things will be given to you as well" (Matthew 6:33).

CHAPTER 8

Working in New Creation Hope

I HAD THE privilege of visiting the famed Notre Dame Cathedral with my wife, Amy, about a month before the devastating 2019 fire that destroyed its spire and roof. Before entering the Gothic gem, we walked around the structure, admiring its massive size and innovative flying buttress design. As we approached the front doors, we gazed up at its two iconic towers, and at the twenty-eight life-size Kings of Judah statues, long-since repaired after their beheadings during the French Revolution in 1793.[105] We stepped inside and wandered around the periphery of the sanctuary, absorbing in awe the place where England's Henry VI was crowned king of France in 1431, and where Napoleon was coronated as emperor in 1804. We felt overwhelmed by the enormity of the space, and the masterfully crafted rib vaulted ceiling, stained-glass rose windows, and eight-thousand-pipe Great Organ. We climbed the 387 steps up the spiral staircase, stopping halfway at the north tower's open gallery to enjoy a close up of the chimera and gargoyles eerily overlooking the city. Next came the south tower belfry, which housed the thirteen-ton Emmanuel bell, one of those made famous in *The Hunchback of Notre Dame*. From there, we had a breathtaking panoramic view of the heart of Paris. It was a transcendent experience.

While taking in the cathedral's beauty, I couldn't help but think of the laborers who built it centuries ago. Workers laid its first stone in 1163, but the structure was not completed until 1345. That's 182 years and eight generations of construction crews.

What would it have been like to spend your days hammering and chiseling stone to meet the specs dictated by your foreman, knowing that neither you, nor your children, nor possibly even your children's children would live to see the final product in all its glory? You would understand it is a special project that will result in something incredible, and that your contributions to it would outlive you, serving as a (possibly literal) foundation on which others would build. I imagined this would give a great deal of meaning to your work now, as you envision the completed cathedral, even while knowing the ultimate realization of your effort, together with the work of the other artisans collaborating on the same goal, would come later.

In the Four-Act Story of Scripture, we are living in the third act—redemption—while anticipating that final renewal when Jesus ushers in the new heavens and the new earth. The work we do now during this third act is like the work of the stonemasons who built Notre Dame—it is intimately and powerfully connected to the fourth act: renewal. N. T. Wright invokes the cathedral-building metaphor to describe this reality: An architect draws up plans and passes them to a group of masons. They get to work, perhaps not knowing precisely how their efforts fit into the completed whole, but trusting the architect and embracing the truth that their efforts will not be wasted. "When the cathedral is complete," explains Wright, "their work will be enhanced, ennobled, will mean much more than it could have meant as they were chiseling it and shaping down in the stonemason's yard."[106] Wright admits the image is incomplete because whereas the cathedral is built by a collection of craftspeople, the new heavens and new earth will be "a fresh gift of transformation and renewal from the Architect himself." In that sense we are building *for* the kingdom, rather than building the kingdom, because God builds God's kingdom. Still, the image illustrates how the work we do in this present life has continuity with the life to come, when God will make all things new in Christ. "The work we do in the present, then," Wright concludes, "gains its full significance from the eventual design in which it is meant to belong."[107]

After laying out Scripture's Four-Act Story foundation, we walked through the process of discerning a calling by attending to the Spirit's direction as revealed in your gifts and the world's needs. We examined the practical question of what works in a job search and explored how to navigate the rapid changes we face in the world of work. As you settle into, or continue in, your career, you will establish good work habits and carry out your work with excellence, with God's help. As you do so, questions about your work's meaning will naturally emerge. When that happens, take a step back and again place the story of your work within the broader context of God's creation-fall-redemption-renewal story. Given what the Bible tells us of God's creative and redemptive work, and his mission to make all things new, how can you work in new creation hope, as God's agent of renewal? Answering this question is key to living your calling in your career—and is the focus of this chapter.

What the Future of Work Means for You Now

To address the question of how best to live out your calling today, start by looking ahead—not just at your five-year plan, or even what lies ahead in your lifetime. Instead, think for a moment about the life to come. After Jesus foretold the destruction of the temple in Jerusalem, his disciples saw an opportunity to ask about this. "Tell us," they said, "when will this happen, and what will be the sign of your coming and of the end of the age?" (Matthew 24:3b).

Jesus's response to their question included a series of para-
bles. One is set within a work environment. Matthew 25:14–30
tells of a man who called three servants together before leaving
on a trip. He entrusted a different portion of his wealth to each
servant for the duration of his travel. "To one he gave five bags
of gold," Jesus said, "to another two bags, and to another one
bag, each according to his ability." Then the man took off. The
servants who received five and three bags of gold, respectively,
invested the money and doubled its value. The third servant
opted to bury his allotment instead. (In that era, burying money
wrapped in cloth was a common way to protect it, and in Jewish
law, a person could not be held liable for the loss of money that
had been buried. It was the easy way out for the third servant.)
After a long time away, their master returned and the servants
converged to settle accounts. To each of the first two, the master
replied, "Well done, good and faithful servant! You have been
faithful with a few things; I will put you in charge of many things.
Come and share your master's happiness!" But to the man who
returned his one bag of gold with no interest, the master said,
"You wicked, lazy servant! . . . You should have put my money on
deposit with the bankers, so that when I returned I would have
received it back with interest. So take the bag of gold from him
and give it to the one who has ten bags. For whoever has will be
given more, and they will have an abundance. Whoever does not
have, even what they have will be taken from them. And throw
that worthless servant outside, into the darkness, where there
will be weeping and gnashing of teeth."

In Jewish thought, God's ownership of his good creation
makes each of us a caretaker or steward of the gifts we've been
entrusted with—our money, our time, our health, our interests/
values/personality/abilities, and the power of the Holy Spirit in
us. The parable stresses our mandate to accept responsibility

for using our gifts in building for the kingdom, for God's glory, rather than squander them out of ambivalence, lack of motivation, or a fear of failure.[108] And remember the context of the parable; it was part of Jesus's response to the disciples' question about his return to earth "at the end of the age." This suggests that our stewardship of our gifts and our faithfulness to our callings today will translate into a new set of responsibilities and opportunities after Christ returns. The story urges us to work in a way that anticipates the kingdom coming in its fullness, faithfully attending to what we're blessed with now. Clearly, our work today matters a great deal. And when Christ returns, we will "share [our] master's happiness," but we will also be blessed with more work to do.[109]

Heaven Will Be a Place on Earth, and We'll Work There

Wait a minute—we'll have work to do in heaven? For many Christians today, this does not quite compute. Most believers surely recognize that the image of angels playing harps while lounging on clouds isn't quite right, but in my experience, many still imagine heaven as a place where believers eternally live out a blissful, disembodied existence somewhere far away, in another dimension utterly separate from our broken world. This vision is popular in Christian consciousness, but it cannot be found anywhere the Bible. Heaven does exist, of course; it is a transcendent part of the created universe (Genesis 1:1), the location of God's throne (with earth as his footstool [Isaiah 66:1–2]), a realm where God's will is perfectly accomplished (Matthew 6:10). But the biblical hope and expectation are that God's salvation will one day fully transform creation when Christ returns to make all things new (Revelation 21:1–5). Our future is here, after heaven comes to earth, and heaven and earth become one.

There is continuity but also discontinuity in how our world today extends into the new creation. In his book *Work Matters*, Tom Nelson explores this theme, noting how the Bible's language in describing the New Jerusalem in Revelation 21 is "very earthy." The text describes walls and gates inlaid with precious metals and gems, like gold, jasper, agate, and turquoise. Yet it is also very different from our current home because the pain and death we experience now will be gone, replaced by radical healing. We will work in the new creation, absolutely, but our work will also be radically healed, no longer toilsome. Reflecting on this future can transform how we think about what we do all day now, granting us meaning and a new sense of creativity and commitment. It allows us to own the Apostle Paul's instruction to "Always give of yourselves fully to the work of the Lord, because you know that your labor in the Lord is not in vain" (1 Corinthians 15:18). As Nelson encourages:

> What you do here is not a waste. The skills and abilities you are developing now in your workplace will not be wasted; they will be utilized and further developed in the future work God has for you to do in the new heavens and the new earth. Your time here in our Father's fallen world is a preparation for an eternity of activity and creativity in the new heavens and new earth. Your work matters not only now but also for the future.[110]

We don't know exactly what our work will look like in the new heavens and the new earth because Scripture offers little detail in describing it. Wright refers to what the Bible teaches about this as a signpost, not a photograph of what we'll experience when we arrive where the signpost points.[111] But these truths can change our attitude from one that equates work with drudgery to one overflowing with creativity and conscientiousness. We should brim with anticipation of our glorious future, overwhelmed with joy, knowing we are working for God's kingdom now.

Making a Biblical View of Work Practical

Whatever work we do, if done for Christ, is not in vain; it will last into eternity. That's the takeaway for this chapter so far. That forthcoming renewal gives meaning to our work today. But the broader context of the Four-Act Story of Scripture gives us additional sources of meaning and purpose in our work. The creation-fall-redemption-renewal framework encourages us to embrace our divinely ordained role as caretakers and cultivators of creation, to identify the ways sin has infected the sphere of influence we manage, and to find ways to help redeem our corners of creation in new creation hope. With this as our collective calling, the three questions we've asked throughout this book should motivate Christians in any and every area of work:

1. What aspects of this area of work are rooted in God's creational design, and therefore need to be preserved, developed, and cultivated?
2. In what ways has this area of work been impacted by the fall, so that it now reflects a distortion of what God intended?
3. What would it look like for this area of work to be fully redeemed (that is, renewed), and what specific things can I do to work toward that?

These three questions help combat alternative narratives to which we have all been conditioned—like the humanist denial of sin and downplaying of anything sacred, the unhelpful sacred/secular distinction that discourages Christians from engaging with the wide expanse of God's creation, and the materialist narrative that defines our personal value by our economic value. The Bible does not address the three questions directly (when they are asked of, say, advertising, or elementary education, or chemistry), but always serves as the scaffold within which they can be explored. To illustrate, imagine an engineer has carefully designed a complex machine that a team of engineering students is assigned to build.[112] Now imagine the engineer left detailed schematics but also written instructions that outline the main purpose of the machine and the ways it will make people's lives better. The students will rely on both the schematics and the written instructions to build the machine. The written instructions are like Scripture, providing big-picture information to guide the task but not the details on every small point. The schematics, serving like the revelation of nature, provide all the specific measurements, diagrams, and many other small details that are clear only with very careful study and experience.

Essentially, the questions to ask in whatever career you are pursuing are as follows: What does Scripture tell you about God's design? How does that fit with what you observe and experience in the details of carrying out the work itself?

Three Examples

Applying the Four-Act Story's transformative vision for work obviously can take some practice.[113] It also helps to see examples of Christians in different fields living it out. The following are three examples of work that orient to God's grand story in

the seemingly varied fields of retail clothing, art, and community development.

Bold socks. Ryan grappled with the three questions noted
above in leading boldSOCKS, a start-up company he joined
just a couple years out of college, and where he now serves as
CEO. The company sells funky socks, which are both functional
and, in some button-down lines of work, offer just about the
only way people can have a little fun expressing themselves. His
work gives Ryan a chance to express his own creativity, since he
has a hand in designing products for the Statement Sockwear
label, the company's in-house sock line. Aesthetic beauty, creativity, self-expression, fun—these are all part of God's original
creation, worthy of being celebrated and enjoyed. But beyond
that, Ryan and his team envisioned a way for a luxury item like
twelve-dollar socks to offer some extra benefit to the world. This
is where some careful analysis is required, because in a fallen
creation, attempts to offer social good sometimes have unin-
tended consequences. For example, Ryan considered a plan
where his company would donate socks to impoverished communities around the globe. The more he studied this option,
though, the more he realized the donated socks would undermine the efforts of local clothing businesses and their wholesale
suppliers to make their living. Plus, what would be left if the
donation program ended? Short-term gain, long-term loss.

Ryan's team sought a more sustainable approach. They set-
tled on providing clean water in regions of Africa where that critical commodity is scarce, through a partnership with 20 Liters,
an organization offering an innovative system of clean water fil-
tration and cisterns. Now each pair of Statement Sockwear pur-
chased provides one hundred days of clean water, saving people
from walking miles to collect it, sparing them from waterborne
illness, and empowering them to invest their gifts in building

businesses within their own communities. The partnership was an ingenious marketing move, a win-win investment that sells more socks and correspondingly supports more communities as they move in the direction of shalom.

The next step for boldSOCKS was to reevaluate how the products were manufactured. Most of us know virtually nothing about how our clothing is produced, but we want it fast and cheap. Meeting the "fast and cheap" demand, though, often means cutting corners throughout the supply chain, compromising quality, treating people unfairly, and disregarding the environment—practices that result in inexpensive clothing, but with sobering trade-offs. This problem kept Ryan awake at night, acutely aware of the effects of sin in his industry. When his team couldn't get answers to all their questions from their manufacturer in Turkey, they looked for a new partnership.

After an exhaustive search, they found what they were looking for in Colombia. A manufacturer there used a vertically integrated supply chain. Instead of having layers of brokers at every step (each contributing to the price), the company's vertical integration strategy allows them to lean on their core values to decide what the manufacturing process looks like from beginning to end, from growing and picking cotton to yarn-spinning to the dying and weaving of a sock. The company reinvests in its labor force, helping workers develop new skills that enhance their career adaptability and make them upwardly mobile. They offer employees subsidized food programs, exercise programs, and scholarships. "That, to us, is ethical manufacturing," Ryan conveyed. This approach takes extra effort and costs a little extra, too, but it's a core strategy for recognizing that businesses can be a force for good, partnering with Christ to confront evil where it is found, and working redemptively to encourage the flourishing of people, communities, and the broader creation—

all in new creation hope. For Ryan, this work capitalizes on his gifts and provides him with unique and tangible opportunities to live out his calling meaningfully, in ways that bring glory to God.

Art of transformation. Christy understands the effects of the fall more viscerally than most. Abuse and neglect were a regular part of her childhood experience, growing up around the poverty line as the youngest of seven in a single-parent household in Mississippi. Uncertainty abounded as her family relocated often. "My childhood was not safe nor stable," she expressed. The experience shaped Christy's relationship with objects. A full-time artist, many of the materials Christy uses in her work are things she inherited from her grandparents or gleaned from their estate, things like an old quilt. The objects have special significance for her, because her grandparents' home served as a safe haven during her family's long summer and Christmas visits. Christy's art builds on the idea that when an object breaks down and falls into disrepair, it can be granted a kind of new life, taking on new functions and opening up, in her words, "a new world of hope."[114]

Christy's work is inspired by other contemporary artists who emphasize the beauty of repair. For example, in her series *Sidewalk Kintsukuroi*,[115] Rachel Sussman gilded cracks in a sidewalk in gold, evoking the traditional Japanese practice of using gold to fill the cracks in broken ceramics. The work draws attention to the damage and the need for repair, but also to the new beauty created when the repair is made. The result is an object more beautiful after the repair than before. The themes of creation, fall, redemption, and renewal are unmistakable in the work, and in Christy's art too. "My work is a gospel story," she said. "I think we're all broken and in need of a Savior, and that's what my work is about." For one of her series, Christy invented an alphabet using images of the various stages of a caterpillar transforming into a butterfly, then used the alphabet to depict, in code, poems she had written about her process of coping with painful experiences from her past. The work conveyed an honest acknowledgment of brokenness covered by a celebration of her healing and an overriding new creation hope.

As a believer, the theme of hope is a reflection of Christy's relationship with Christ. Her work helps her cope with her own pain and draws her nearer to the One in whom she has new life. But it also serves as a healing salve for the wounds of other survivors of abuse. "My practice hopes to take some of the hard work and time that I have invested as a survivor and offer it visually to others," she shared.

> By subtly, or not so subtly, creating an opening for conversation, art allows my voice to enter a dialogue that is often too hard to join with actual words. . . . This communication might not be a straightforward one, but I think it is my faith in the essence of art that encourages me to try to translate the hope of healing and growth to others. I offer my artwork as a visual and experiential interaction to increase the capacity for empathy toward individuals who have survived wounds, especially those who work diligently for a lifetime in order to heal.[116]

Flourishing neighborhoods. Brianna's first gig after college was through AmeriCorps in Milwaukee, doing neighborhood audits, cataloguing community strengths, and kicking off improvement projects designed with input from neighbors. She studied art and engineering in college "without intentions of being an artist or engineer," she said. As a child, she envisioned building things and spent hour after hour sketching elaborate houses and living spaces. Ultimately, her interest in architecture led to her urban planning, which in turn led her to community development—still building but building strength-based community cultures rather than physical structures.

Her AmeriCorps experience prepared Brianna for a position with a community development nonprofit in Milwaukee. As she carries out the work—now as the organization's executive director—she often reflects on the challenges and opportunities of living in the "already but not yet" space in which Christ's kingdom has been established but is not yet here in its fullness. "We know things are not the way God intended," Brianna expressed.

But how do we work toward a vision of human flourishing, in relationship with God? Our organization focuses in three main areas—one is housing, one is economic development, one is grassroots leadership development. We want to ensure that people have access to opportunity and that people are equipped with knowledge, skills, and resources. Many folks in the neighborhood are first-generation immigrants, thinking about housing opportunities but not knowing much about how to navigate the system, how to get bank loans, etc. So part of our work is to ask what people are dreaming of and help them navigate the system while also working to improve the system to make it more just for all people.

Much of Brianna's work builds on God's creational design of people as relational beings, thriving when living in supportive relationships. "It goes back to human flourishing in community together," she said. "There is an element of relationship with God being a triune God. We are meant to live in relationship with each other. Flourishing comes through that. A lot of the work we do here is to connect people to one another, sometimes by starting at a block party. That builds a sense of safety, a sense of 'home,' a kind of connectedness and mutuality. Who is your neighbor? That question is addressed often in Scripture." But Brianna also feels the effects of the fall through economic injustices that hamper her community's ability to thrive.

> When we look historically at why things aren't better here, we see problems on multiple levels, but it's clear there are injustices perpetuated by larger systems and abuses of power—an issue that Jesus spoke to quite often. For example, often we see policies that benefit folks who already have money and power. They are able to open businesses but then take the money out of the community rather than reinvesting it here. Then as housing prices rise, people can no longer afford to live here. Where is the justice in that?

The challenges are complex, but Brianna maintains new creation hope. "I love to see people in the neighborhood running their own businesses, reinvesting in the community, and caring for one another. That is the positive vision. I've seen countless examples of kingdom-like economics where neighbors pool together their skills, talents, and resources to help one another repair their homes, open businesses, and feed one another delicious meals. When we're all caring for our neighbor we can live into that flourishing. I hope my work contributes to that."

Your Work Matters

Ryan, Christy, and Brianna are living their callings in very different professions, each of them embracing their role as cultivators of creation, each of them acutely aware of the effects of the fall within their spheres of influence, each of them working redemptively in new creation hope. How about you? What is God's creational design for the career path to which you are called? How have the effects of the fall distorted or hampered your area of work? What possibilities do you see for working toward redemption in anticipation of the new heavens and the new earth? Whatever your area of work, be reminded: what you do in the Lord is not in vain. I cannot describe your work's significance better than N. T. Wright:

> You are not oiling the wheels of a machine that's about to roll over a cliff. You are not restoring a great painting that is shortly going to be thrown in the fire. You are not planting roses in a garden that's about to be dug up for a building site. You are—strange though it may seem, almost as hard to believe as the resurrection itself—accomplishing something that will become in due course part of God's new world. Every act of love, gratitude, and kindness; every work of art or music inspired by the love of God and delight in the beauty of his creation; every minute spent teaching a severely handicapped child to read or to walk; every act of care and nurture, of comfort and support, for one's fellow human beings and for that matter one's fellow non-human creatures; and of course every prayer, all Spirit-led teaching, every deed that spreads the

gospel, builds up the church, embraces and embodies holiness rather than corruption, and makes the name of Jesus honored in the world—all of this will find its way, though the resurrecting power of God, into the new creation that God will one day make. That is the logic of the mission of God. God's re-creation of his wonderful world, which began with the resurrection of Jesus and continues mysteriously as God's people live in the risen Christ and in the power of his Spirit, means that what we do in Christ and by the Spirit in the present is not wasted. It will last all the way into God's new world. In fact, it will be enhanced there.[117]

Psychologists who study well-being in career development suggest three things are needed for work to be meaningful.[118] The first is *coherence*; that is, the work needs to make sense. You need to understand what your work is accomplishing. The second is *purpose*; that is, you need to have a sense of direction, some core goals for your work. Third, you need a sense of *significance*, to feel that your work matters, that it contributes something of value to the world. My hope is that after reading this book, these three criteria are easy for you to identify in your career. Social scientists can demonstrate that when your experience at work aligns with your global meaning system, good outcomes result. Coherence, purpose, and significance are good for people; this is how God made us. But these criteria take on added significance for believers who find alignment not just between their work and their own personal stories but between their work and God's grand story too. As Christians, our work makes sense because we can place ourselves and our careers within the broader context of God's creation-fall-redemption-renewal story. Our work's purpose is defined by how we express our gifts through our work for God's glory and make the world better. And our significance is profoundly rooted in the good we do today by cultivating creation, thwarting the effects of sin, partnering in Christ's redemptive work—and even more so by working in new creation hope. We are God's agents of renewal in the world, so even into eternity, our work absolutely matters. Your work absolutely matters. Take it to heart.

The Four-Act Story of Scripture:
Our Foundation for Redeeming Work

THROUGHOUT THIS BOOK, I've referred to the Bible as a story spanning four acts—creation, fall, redemption, and renewal. I've contrasted this Four-Act Story with a Two-Act Story view, the sin-and-salvation narrative that focuses narrowly on fall and redemption, a prevailing perspective among Christians today. Christians who keep all four acts in mind and approach their work accordingly experience tremendous joy, purpose, and meaning as a result. That is the case not because human happiness is the end goal of the Bible's story, as the Two-Act Story implies. Rather, it flows naturally from our recognition that God has redeemed and will fully renew his fallen creation, and God chooses to use us to help make this happen. We are God's agents of renewal. What could possibly make work more meaningful and purpose-driven than that?

Yet the Four-Act Story seems all too elusive among Christians today. Even Christians who have embraced the Four-Act Story often find themselves drifting into Two-Act Story thinking, unconsciously parsing the world into sacred and secular spheres. Doubling down on the Four-Act Story is crucial for a fully integrative faith and work life, which is why everything in this book has built on a Four-Act Story foundation. In chapter 1, I painted a broad-stroke picture of the four acts. This appendix offers more detail. Let's dig into each of the four acts, in turn.

Creation

All Christians acknowledge God as creator and sustainer of the universe. The first verse in the Bible reads, "In the beginning, God created the heavens and the earth." Not only did God bring into being the universe and all that is in it, but throughout the first chapter of Genesis, "God saw that it was good."

By any measure, we'd have to agree that "good" is putting it mildly. It is overwhelming to consider the vast expanse of the cosmos; the part that humans can observe allows us to detect its outer edges at somewhere around 13.8 billion light-years away. That's just the part that, theoretically, we can see; the entire universe is conservatively estimated to span 7 trillion light-years from one end to the other.[119] The observable universe alone contains somewhere between 200 billion to 2 trillion galaxies.[120] One of these is our modest home, the Milky Way galaxy, which contains somewhere in the ballpark of 1 trillion stars.[121] How can our finite minds even begin to grasp the magnitude of these numbers, and the volume of space they represent?

On the other end of the creational continuum, a typical atom—the tiniest unit of ordinary matter—is roughly one ten-billionth of a meter in size. Line up about 1 million carbon atoms, for example, and you've got the width of a human hair.[122] I think about these differences in scope, and I am overcome with a sense of awe, a different version of the same kind of breathtaking awe I experience when taking in a brilliant, bright-orange sunset over the Rocky Mountains near my home. The divine creativity involved in bringing such varied wonders into being is just as hard to fathom. I can imagine ladybugs and cockroaches and flies and bees and butterflies and (ugh) mosquitoes, but nine hundred thousand different kinds of insects?[123] Then consider the elegant interdependencies of diverse species within ecosystems, in which certain environments allow certain types (but not other types!) of plants and animal life to thrive in concert together. Next, think about the form and function of the different parts of just one species—say, humans. Choose an anatomical system and marvel at the manner in which the different organs function together like a symphony to accomplish all of the tasks of sustaining life. Finally, reflect on the invisible laws that govern all these things, that give them order and consistency, and that make science possible as a way of knowing. You get the picture. The natural world, God's handiwork, is utterly, almost incomprehensibly, amazing.

And creation is more than amazing—it is *revelatory*. That is, God reveals himself in creation, as he does in Scripture, a point eloquently expressed in Psalm 19: "The heavens declare the glory of God; the skies proclaim the work of his hands. Day after day they pour forth speech; night after night they reveal knowledge" (vv. 1–2). God's eternal power and divine nature are clearly seen in creation (Romans 1:20), which means that when we experience, study, and enjoy creation, we are learning about God, God's nature, and what God cares about.[124]

The beauty, promise, and value in creation are not limited to the natural world, either. This is where humans come in; we play a special role in this story. In Genesis 1, we read that God resolved to create humankind "in our own image." God did so, blessed them, and then gave them these instructions: "Be fruitful and increase in number; fill the earth and subdue it. Rule over the fish in the sea and the birds in the sky and over every living creature that moves on the ground" (v. 28). This famous verse, the poetic climax of the creation story, is known as the "creation mandate" or the "cultural mandate." Following this command is not the only way that we bear God's image, but it's an extremely important way as it applies to our work. To "be fruitful and increase in number" means to develop the cultural possibilities that are latent in the raw material of creation, to create culture and all that comes with it: families and churches, art and architecture, language and laws, cities and economic structures. To "subdue" the earth means to coax out creation's potentialities—in agriculture, design, education, commerce, and technology. God's creation was, and is, brimming with promise and possibility. With this in mind, work is way more than merely a way to pay the bills. "Our work is an honor," writes Richard Pratt, "a privileged commission from our great King. God has given each of us a portion of his kingdom to explore and to develop to its fullness."[125]

It's worth pausing here and pointing out a couple of things. First, note that humans receive this instruction before sin enters the world. Some Christians, aware of Genesis 3 (e.g., v. 17: "Cursed is the ground because of you; through painful toil you will eat food from it"), seem to assume that work is bad, part of the penalty for our sin. Not so. Work became toilsome as a result of the fall, but just as God himself worked in his act of creation, so humans were charged (or rather, blessed) with work to do prior to the fall. In Genesis 2:15, for example, Adam was placed in the Garden of Eden "to work it and take care of it." This is a metaphor for our own work. We image God by developing his creation in creative ways, and also by caring for it. Second, historically, some Christians have interpreted the command to "rule over" creation in ways that have led them to exploit it, approaching it with an attitude of conquest. This abhorrent response to the text clearly runs counter to its intention. Instead, to "rule over" (alternatively, to "have dominion") should be read in the sense of stewardship. "In the kingdom of God," writes theologian Neal Plantinga, "to have dominion is to care for the well-being of others . . . to act like the mediator of creation . . . [to] give creation room to be itself . . . [to] respect it, care for it, empower it . . . [to] live in healthy interdependence with it."[126] Creation has been entrusted to us, and we're called to serve not as conquerors but caretakers and cultivators.

Let's summarize: God created everything. Creation is very good. Humans are created in God's image. A big part of being an image-bearer means taking care of creation, stewarding it, and developing it in ways that bring out its God-given potential.

Christians who operate according to a Two-Act Story recognize that God created everything, but they fail to fully integrate the creation mandate into how they think about their work. A more expansive view of creation makes clear that living out one's faith at work means much more than working toward saving souls (although to be clear: it is wonderful when God uses us to achieve that goal). It means also embracing the reality that all of creation is God's, and all of it is entrusted to us to care for and cultivate, with God's help and for God's glory. The implications here are profound, and they apply to everyone, in every career field. Think about the work that you do, or that you're considering doing. What is God's creational design for that sphere of culture? What does it mean for you to care for or develop your corner of creation, however large or small it is, within your career?

Fall

Discussing creation in light of the first two chapters of Genesis, before getting to Genesis 3, always feels a bit divorced from reality, almost naïve. Some cultural optimists believe we are on a trajectory toward perfection, that people are basically good and self-correcting, and that technology and enlightenment will eventually lead to self-actualization for people and for the world. This is a different kind of two-act story, one that fails to retain the good news of the gospel at all. This story either denies the effects of sin and the need for a savior entirely, or it minimizes the effects of sin and looks for redemption in all the wrong places. If we look at our own experience, we know better. We sin, and we suffer the effects of sin everywhere we turn. I often tell people that when it comes to understanding theology, the doctrine of total depravity[127] has always seemed the most obvious to me; I need go no further than my own self to see it.

Genesis 3 details Adam and Eve's fall into sin, fueled by their desire to be like God, instead of embracing their ordained role as his servants. The Two-Act Story emphasizes how their disobedience introduced sin into the world, forever leaving the human condition broken and in need of healing. And rightly so; we feel the weight of our own sin like an ache deep in our bones, and deep in our psyches. Yet the impact of sin is much broader than the chasm it creates between people and God. Just as the goodness of Creation is exhaustive in scope, so are the effects of the fall. Al Wolters puts it powerfully:

> Adam and Eve's fall into sin was not just an isolated act of disobedience but an event of catastrophic significance for creation as a whole. Not only the whole human race but the whole nonhuman world too was caught up in the train of Adam's failure to heed God's explicit commandment and warning. The effects of sin touch all of creation; no created thing is in principle untouched by the corrosive effects of the fall. Whether we look at societal structures such as the state or family, or cultural pursuits such as art or technology, or bodily functions such as sexuality or eating, or anything at all within the wide scope of creation,

we discover that the good handiwork of God has been drawn into the sphere of human mutiny against God. "The whole creation," Paul writes in a profound passage of Romans, "has been groaning as in the pains of childbirth right up to the present time" (Rom. 8:22).[128]

We experience the effects of sin regularly in our daily grind. In fact, the effects of sin are what make our work so often a "daily grind" in the first place. Misunderstandings among coworkers and customers abound, and relationships are strained. Greed results in price-gouging and insider trading. Good art is thwarted by kitsch and commercialism. Industrial waste, disposed of irresponsibly, poisons our environment. Resources are scarce in some places and hoarded in others, and social consequences are denied or downplayed. Oppressive barriers limit opportunities for classes of people on the basis of things outside of their control, like how their names sound or what they look like. Efforts to reach our organizations' financial goals sometimes leave the most precarious workers disproportionally vulnerable, without us even noticing. I could go on, but you get the point. Too much of our work is marred by suffering, alienation, conflict, futility, frustration, pain, and disappointment. Things are simply not the way they are supposed to be.[129]

That sense that things are not the way they are supposed to be is how sin and evil work. We experience good creation gone awry, tainted and distorted by the effects of evil. These effects are obvious in our personal lives and in human affairs, but the nonhuman world is subject to it as well. "The very soil is affected by Adam's sin, making agriculture more difficult,"[130] writes Wolters, referring to Genesis 3:17—all as a result of human guilt. Yet while sin distorts creation, by God's grace it does not fundamentally undermine the created goodness that remains in the world. For example, unsustainable farming practices that over-rely on harm-inducing chemicals in search of high yields often reflect callous greed, but the cultural goodness of cultivating the land to feed communities is still in place. Similarly, pornography, prostitution, and human trafficking are built on heartless exploitation that shatters the healthy expression of sexuality, yet the created goodness of sexuality remains. Sin does not undo God's good handiwork, but deforms it, like a parasite on his creational design.

The Christian response to the effects of sin on creation has not always been great. All too often, Christians have sensed the taint of sin in the world and retreated, fleeing from sin but also from the created goodness that sin has twisted. Jesus taught that "My kingdom is not of this world" (John 18:36); Paul implored believers, "Do not conform any longer to the pattern of this world" (Romans 12:2); and James noted that pure and faultless religion includes one's efforts "to keep oneself from being polluted by the world" (1:27). These passages seem pretty clear, except that the "world" in each passage means those places where sin has infected creation; it does not refer to creation itself. This is a subtle but very important point because over the centuries and still today, some Christians have declared that certain swaths of culture are "worldly" and therefore ought to be avoided, whereas others are holy and pure and appropriate for Christian involvement. The result is the kind of separation of life into sacred and secular spheres described in several places in this book; some areas of life (like the work of the church) are sacred, and others (everything else) are secular. This way of thinking is a stubborn holdover from the ancient Greek world-view, which argued that the life of the mind is the purest form of being, and anything that interfered with that (like the work of our hands) disrupts progress toward that kind of purity. In the

Christian church, monasteries were set up to allow those "called to a religious vocation" to devote dedicated time to prayer and the study of Scriptures, free from worldly distractions. While monasteries still exist, many Christians operating outside of the cloister retain the same basic perspective, only they believe what they do on Sunday to be sacred, while the rest of the week is, at best, religiously neutral. That was certainly the case in the room at that Fusing Faith and Life conference described in chapter 1.

A tragic consequence of this sacred/secular distinction is that whole generations of Christians have been taught to avoid some areas of creation, like the film industry, academic scholarship, biological science, or politics. But biblical warnings against worldliness do not mean avoiding spheres of creation where sin exists; if that were the case, Christians would have no options at all—including work within the church. Ironically, many Christians who have argued against engagement in "secular" pursuits also cry out against the increasing secularism in the culture. They largely have themselves to blame. Seeing it coming, many Christians still step aside and let secularism unfold, lest they be tainted by it. As a result, with few believers on the front lines of culture to stem the tide, the rise of secularism has only picked up its pace. The Bible does not teach that some areas of creation are secular and others are sacred. Rather, all of life is sacred because all of it was created by God. However, all of it also has been tainted by sin—sin that should be opposed wherever it is found.

Even while still retaining its created goodness, "the whole creation groans" and cries out for redemption. In what ways do you notice (or anticipate) this in your work? How have the effects of the fall infected God's creational design within your profession, or within the career path you are considering?

Redemption

As the book of Genesis continues, we read of a God who showers his people with grace and mercy. This gospel of grace doesn't start in the New Testament, but in the midst of the curse in Genesis 3:15, when God alludes to a coming savior who will crush the serpent's head. Then God seeks out his children, and in verse 21, he clothes them to provide relief from the shame they feel because of their sin. In doing so, he warms them with, as Plantinga puts it, "mercy in a world grown chilly from their own sin. God outfits humans with durable clothing they should never have needed—a piece of kindness that launches the history of God's grace from Genesis to Revelation."[131] God's grace continues in his rescue of Noah in Genesis 6–8, and in his "everlasting covenant" with Noah and his family in Genesis 9. It continues in his calling of Abram, and in his "everlasting covenant" with Abram in Genesis 15—another promise for the whole world of God's faithfulness. The story proceeds with Hagar and Ishmael, Isaac and Rebekah, Jacob and Esau, Moses and the exodus out of Egypt. Children's Bible storybooks, perhaps inspired by Hebrews 11, often frame these stories as a journey through the hall of faith heroes, women and men who do serve as good (though far from perfect) role models. Yet the real hero is God, and the real story is his unbroken, unceasing faithfulness, mercy, and grace. As these stories are told, the one constant is God's unwavering commitment to keep his covenant with people who constantly break it.

After the exodus, as God's people are wandering in the desert, he renews his covenant of grace with Moses, whose role as mediator of Israel's redemption points to the more perfect "Moses" yet to come. Then God laid down the law, as it were, giving Moses the Ten Commandments. This happens after God had rescued his people from slavery; importantly, they were called to obey the law not to earn that rescue but as a response to the fact that it had already been granted. Of course, God's people regularly fail to obey his law. Plantinga masterfully summarizes how the Old Testament unfolds from there:

> The pages of the Old Testament give us not only the wisdom of Solomon and the psalms of David; not only the faithfulness of Samuel and the patience of Job; but also a sequence of macho judges, wicked kings, false prophets, and unholy priests. King David himself— simultaneously godly and corrupt—shows us what God must deal with. God loves his people . . . but God hates the sin that keeps dragging his people backward toward slavery. . . . So by way of the "latter prophets" (Isaiah through Malachi), God warns of coming disaster. Almost desperately, the prophets call people to return to God. But the people of God "have a stubborn and rebellious heart" that will not face facts. "No one repents of wickedness, saying, 'What have I done!'" (Jer. 8:6). In response to such stubbornness, the God of the prophets sounds weary at times, exasperated at the perversity of people who worship piously and also chisel their neighbors. Exodus, law, prophets, priests, kings—seemingly none of these can stop the shipwreck of Israel and her mission to the nations.[132]

Through it all, God bears with great love and patience the stubbornness of his people, who continually disappoint and fail to repent. Prophets speak of God's judgment and they warn of the impending Babylonian exile, but they also look ahead to God's salvation, when he will set people free once again. The prophets also long, just as we do today, for a time when all things are made new—when people finally cast away their sin, when pain and suffering cease, when promises are kept and relationships are restored. This describes shalom, a deep sense of peace in which all things are the way they are supposed to be. The prophets heard God's voice and offered assurance that his kingdom of shalom would indeed come one day, and that a Messiah would usher it in.

That Messiah, of course, is Jesus Christ. God's people yearned for a Savior but expected something different than what they got, probably a political or military hero who would lead their rise to power and provide relief from the pressing thumb of Rome. Instead, their Messiah came in the humblest fashion, born in a stable and laid in a manger, raised in Nazareth as the son of a craftsman. He was not a political king at all, yet he was the King of kings, God incarnate: Immanuel, or God-with-us. "Though he was God, he did not think of equality with God as something to cling to," wrote the Apostle Paul. "Instead, he gave up his divine privileges; he took the humble position of a slave and was born as a human being. When he appeared in human form, he humbled himself in obedience to God and died a criminal's death on a cross" (Philippians 2:6–8 NLT).[133] Jesus lived like a repentant sinner even though he never sinned. He endured rebuke, accusation, mockery, and humiliation, all the way to his death by crucifixion. Why? He gave "his life as a ransom for many" (Mark 10:45), and as "the atoning sacrifice for our sins" (1 John 4:10) because humans are deeply flawed, totally incapable of atoning for our own sins. He paid the penitent price for the sins of the world, the only one who could (yet the least deserving), in the ultimate act of grace. He died, and was buried.

On the third day, he rose again from the dead—a miracle, the single most important event in the history of the world, and the very basis of the Christian faith. Jesus's resurrection is the reason that Christians live in hope. For believers, the resurrection guarantees our personal salvation. But more than that: it guarantees the redemption and renewal of the whole creation. "For all of God's promises have been fulfilled in Christ with a resounding 'Yes!'" (2 Corinthians 1:20, NLT). Redemption in Christ addresses the entire scope of the fall. "His resurrection brings the renewed possibility of shalom between humans and God, within humans themselves, among humans, and between humans and the created order," writes Amy Sherman, as I noted in chapter 1. "His redemption has accomplished nothing less than the promise of a restored paradise where shalom in all its dimensions will reign."[134] Redemption, in other words, is cosmic in scope—every bit as exhaustive in impact as the effects of the fall, and every bit as wide-ranging as creation itself.

Note that redemption promises a renewal of God's created intent, not a replacement of it. Redemption means to buy back, to make free again, like releasing a prisoner from bondage or paying the ransom to gain back a child who has been kidnapped. In Christ's redemption, God is not scuttling his earlier creation and starting over. Instead, he is salvaging the original. And humankind? Although we failed miserably in carrying out the creation mandate, Christ's redemption gives us another chance. "We are reinstated as God's managers on earth," writes Wolters. What does this mean for us? Wolters continues:

> The practical implications . . . are legion. Marriage should not be avoided by Christians, but sanctified. Emotions should not be repressed, but purified. Sexuality is not simply to be shunned, but redeemed. Art ought not to be pronounced worldly, but claimed for Christ. Business must no longer be relegated to the

secular world, but must be made to conform again to God-honoring standards. Every sector of human life yields such examples.[135]

Every sector of human life obviously includes every sector of the world of work. Colossians 1 affirms the full expanse of redemption by telling us that "God was pleased to have all his fullness dwell in [Christ], and through him to reconcile to himself *all things*, whether things on earth or things in heaven, by making peace through his blood, shed on the cross" (vv. 19–20, emphasis added). And 2 Corinthians 5:18 tells us that "All this is from God, who reconciled us to himself through Christ and gave us the ministry of reconciliation" as "Christ's ambassadors." Wolters pulls these verses together:

> If Christ is the reconciler of all things, and if we have been entrusted with "the ministry of reconciliation" on his behalf, then we have a redemptive task wherever our vocation places us in his world. No invisible dividing line within creation limits the applicability of such basic biblical concepts as reconciliation, redemption, salvation, sanctification, renewal, the kingdom of God, and so on. In the name of Christ, distortion must be opposed everywhere—in the kitchen and the bedroom, in city councils and corporate boardrooms, on the stage and on the air, in the classroom and in the workshop. Everywhere creation calls for the honoring of God's standards. Everywhere humanity's sinfulness disrupts and deforms. Everywhere Christ's victory is pregnant with defeat of sin and the recovery of creation.[136]

To be sure, God doesn't *need* us to serve as Christ's ambassadors, as if he is somehow unable to usher in the fullness of his kingdom on his own. He is God after all—sovereign, omnipotent, fully in control, and fully in charge. In his wisdom, though, he calls us to play a role in his kingdom work. It truly is hard to imagine anything making our work more meaningful than this. Whatever your sphere of influence, however large or small that may be, what does its redemption in Christ have in store for it? And given the ways it has been impacted by the effects of sin, how can you help make that happen?

Renewal

Christians personally experience the forgiveness and freedom that come from faith in Christ. And we live in new creation hope because his death and resurrection guarantee that all things will be made new. Yet while Jesus taught that "the kingdom of God is among you" (Luke 17:21), he also taught us to pray "your kingdom come" (Luke 11:2). So the kingdom is already here, but it is not yet here in its fullness. Already and not yet. This fits with our reality; we experience a taste of the kingdom in our own hearts and lives, but we do not yet experience it fully. That full and perfect renewal will come when Christ returns, and we long for it. But until that day arrives, we recognize that "all authority in heaven and earth" has already been given to Jesus (Matthew 28:18); he is sovereign over all of it. With the help of the Holy Spirit, we now serve as Christ's hands and feet, working to advance the kingdom everywhere.

Renewal, therefore, refers to where things are headed. That it will come is not a question, because redemption guaranteed it. And while we yearn for that day to come, we don't do so passively. We are saved for a purpose, and our purpose is to partner with

Christ in his "ministry of reconciliation" in whatever sphere to which we are called. For inspiration we can read the book of Revelation, which paints a word-picture of what renewal will entail: a new heaven and a new earth, the New Jerusalem coming down out of heaven, with God seated on his throne, dwelling now among his people. "He will wipe every tear from their eyes," writes John. "There will be no more death or mourning or crying or pain, for the old order of things has passed away" (Revelation 21:4). The "old order" refers to sin and its effects on creation, which will be finally renewed as God intended: "He who was seated on the throne said, 'I am making everything new!'" (v. 5). Revelation 22 continues, describing "the river of the water of life, as clear as crystal, flowing from the throne of God and of the Lamb down the middle of the street of the city. On each side of the river [stands] the tree of life, bearing . . . fruit . . . and the leaves of the tree are for the healing of the nations. No longer will there be any curse. The throne of God and of the Lamb will be in the city, and his servants will serve him. They will see his face, and his name will be on their foreheads" (vv. 1–4).

The fact that the Bible starts in a garden but ends in a garden city should not be lost on us. When Christ returns and all things are made new, we do not return to the Garden of Eden. People were given the mandate to fill the earth and subdue it, develop its potential and build culture. All that effort is not in vain; it is not scrapped and replaced, but rather perfected and renewed. Some Christians object to this claim, pointing to the instruction in 2 Peter 3:10 that "the day of the Lord will come like a thief. The heavens will disappear with a roar; the elements will be destroyed by fire, and the earth and everything done in it will be laid bare." But throughout Scripture, fire is described as a means of purification, not annihilation. And Peter refers to "a new heaven and a new earth" in verse 13 of that chapter, using the Greek word that means "renewed" rather than "brand new."[137] The fire Peter describes is a refining fire that burns off the impurity of sin.[138] God does not forsake the work of his hands; in his faithfulness, he upholds his created order, only makes it new. That is where the course of history is headed—to a renewed, radically healed[139] world. That is what we have to look forward to. It is what God is using our work for, today.

Notes

INTRODUCTION

1. David W. Miller, PhD, director of Princeton University's Faith and Work Initiative, even suggests we are living in the Faith at Work Era. See David W. Miller, *God at Work: The History and Promise of the Faith and Work Movement* (New York: Oxford University Press, 2007).

2. Pete Hammond, R. Paul Stevens, and Todd Svanoe, *The Marketplace Annotated Bibliography: A Christian Guide to Books on Work, Business, and Vocation* (Downers Grove, IL: InterVarsity Press, 2002).

CHAPTER 1

3. Portions of this summary are adapted from an article I wrote for *The Banner*, "Where in the World (of Work) Have All the Reformers Gone?" January 18, 2011, https://thebanner.org/departments/2011/01/where-in-the-world-of-work-have-all-the-reformers-gone.

4. Social psychologist Crystal Park suggests that people experience positive health and well-being when their global worldview beliefs harmonize with their day-to-day experiences in life, including at the workplace. See Crystal L. Park, "Religious and Spiritual Aspects of Meaning in the Context of Work Life," in *Psychology of Religion and Workplace Spirituality*, ed. Peter Hill and Bryan Dik (Charlotte, NC: Information Age, 2012), 25–42.

5. Augustine used the creation-fall-redemption/renewal framework to structure the second half of his *City of God*. Other theologians (e.g., Plantinga, Wolters), like Augustine, combine redemption and renewal into one theme, although the meaning and impact are the same as that achieved using the four acts that I describe here, taking a cue from Stephen Graves. See Cornelius Plantinga Jr., *Engaging God's World: A Reformed Vision of Faith, Learning, and Living* (Grand Rapids: Eerdmans, 2002); Albert M. Wolters, *Creation Regained: Biblical Basics for Reformational Worldview*, 2nd ed. (Grand Rapids: Eerdmans, 2005); Stephen Graves, *The Gospel Goes to Work* (Fayetteville, AR: KJK Inc., 2015). Most

commentators suggest that N. T. Wright was the first to illustrate the story of Scripture using the model of a play. His approach identified five acts: creation, fall, Israel, Jesus, and the rest of the New Testament. See N. T. Wright, "How Can the Bible Be Authoritative?" *Vox Evangelica* 21 (1991), 7–32. Others have described it as chapters in a book (e.g., Whelchel) to the same effect. One might also describe the Bible as a drama with six acts: creation; fall; God's covenantal resolution to crush sin; Jesus's life, ministry, death, and resurrection; the "era of witness" by the church; and restoration/consummation/renewal, as do Michael Goheen and Craig Bartholemew, *The True Story of the Whole World* (Grand Rapids: Faith Alive, 2009). Hugh Whelchel, *All Things New: Rediscovering the Four-Chapter Gospel* (McLean, VA: Institute for Faith, Work & Economics, 2016).

6. Some of the language in this summary of the Four-Act Story, and in the reasons a Two-Act Story falls short, borrows from a helpful booklet by Hugh Whelchel, *All Things New: Rediscovering the Four-Chapter Gospel* (McLean, VA: Institute for Faith, Work & Economics, 2016).

7. Christians don't agree on *how* creation unfolded, but they agree that God is the creator. The curious but uninitiated on this debate might try as a starting point J. B. Stump, ed., *Four Views on Creation, Evolution, and Intelligent Design* (Grand Rapids: Zondervan, 2017).

8. Amy Sherman, *Kingdom Calling: Vocational Stewardship for the Common Good* (Downers Grove, IL: IVP Books, 2011), 78, 79.

9 Short-term missions usually have a positive impact on the people who serve. They provide a potentially life-changing way to bond with other believers in learning about what people experience in other communities, sometimes in other parts of the world. That said, there is substantial debate about their long-term impact on communities that are being served, especially when factoring in the costs of such trips and the alternative options for using those resources to support more sustainable local efforts in the locales that receive them. See Steve Corbett and Brian Fikkert, *When Helping Hurts: How to Alleviate Poverty Without Hurting the Poor... and Yourself,* (Chicago: Moody Publishers, 2014), but also Tracy Kuperus and Roland Hoksbergen, *When Helping Heals* (Grand Rapids: Calvin College Press, 2017).

10. Sharing our faith is an important response to the great commission, our command from Jesus to "make disciples of all nations" (Matthew 28:19).

11. Any type of work can be pursued in this manner, but it is important to recognize as well that in a fallen world, oppression, poverty, and abuses of power on the part of employers can strip work of its dignity.

As Ryan Duffy and I described in our book *Make Your Job a Calling*, there is at least anecdotal evidence that some people in extremely difficult circumstances can nevertheless derive meaning from the work, but this in no way lets employers off the hook from their responsibility to provide "decent work" that affords adequate compensation, hours that afford free time and rest, and a physically and psychologically safe work environment.

12. An excellent interview with Jen is available at the *All Things New* podcast: https://summitview.com/blog/faith-work-jen-dekorte/.

13. Romans 8:22: "We know that the whole creation has been groaning as in the pains of childbirth right up to the present time."

14. The Bible describes itself as God's inspired, authoritative word, "useful for teaching, rebuking, correcting, and training in righteousness, so that the servant of God may be thoroughly equipped for every good work" (2 Timothy 3:16).

15. People didn't ask this question in biblical times. Men inherited their professions. Women married young, had children, and took care of their homes and families. No one explored their options during high school and college before choosing a path to pursue after graduation. It's a very common question today, however—and one with which many people struggle mightily. According to a Barna poll, nearly half of adults are afraid of making the wrong career choice, and just 20 percent have a sense of what God wants them to do with their lives. See Bob Goff, *Multi-Careering: Do Work That Matters at Every Stage of Your Journey* (Grand Rapids: Zondervan, 2013).

16. By "empirical study" here, I mean any research study that applied the methods of science to investigate the concept.

17. See Bryan J. Dik and Ryan D. Duffy, "Calling and Vocation at Work: Definitions and Prospects for Research and Practice," *Counseling Psychologist* 37 (2009), 424–450.

18. Bryan J. Dik, Brandy M. Eldridge, Michael F. Steger, and Ryan D. Duffy, "Development and Validation of the Calling and Vocation Questionnaire (CVQ) and Brief Calling Scale (BCS)," *Journal of Career Assessment* 20 (2012), 242–263.

19. As of 2020, more than five hundred articles and chapters have been published on calling in the social sciences. The following articles and chapters offer detailed, recent reviews of this research: Bryan J. Dik and Ryan D. Duffy, "Strategies for Discerning and Living a Calling," in *APA Handbook of Career Intervention, Volume 2: Applications,* ed. Paul J. Hartung, Mark L. Savickas, and W. Bruce Walsh (Washington, DC:

American Psychological Association, 2015), 305–317; Bryan J. Dik, Adelyn B. Shimizu, Kaitlyn Reed, Dylan R. Marsh, and Jessica Morse, "Career Calling and Career Development," in *International Handbook of Career Guidance*, ed. Harsha Perera and James Athanasou (New York: Springer, forthcoming); Ryan D. Duffy and Bryan J. Dik, "Research on Calling: What Have We Learned and Where Are We Going?" *Journal of Vocational Behavior* 83 (2013), 428–436; Ryan D. Duffy, Bryan J. Dik, Richard P. Douglass, Jessica W. England, and Brandon L. Velez, "Work as a Calling: A Theoretical Model," *Journal of Counseling Psychology* 65 (2018), 423–439; Jeffery A. Thompson and J. Stuart Bunderson, "Research on Work as a Calling . . . and How to Make It Matter," *Annual Review of Organizational Psychology and Organizational Behavior* 6 (2019), 421–443.

20. Micah J. White, Dylan R. Marsh, Bryan J. Dik and Cheryl L. Beseler, "Calling's Prevalence in the United States: Results from a Nationally Representative Sample," (manuscript in preparation, 2020).

CHAPTER 2

21. One of his posts, for example, called out a short-lived Evangelical campaign to boycott Starbucks for its "war on Christmas" (Remember that year they used plain red coffee cups?). It was viewed more than three hundred thousand times (https://nathanielscottlake.wordpress.com /2015/11/08/why-merrychristmasstarbucks-is-everything-wrong-with -american-christianity/).

22. Nathaniel S. Lake, "Playing Out the Christian Faith: Applying a Reformational Worldview to Athletics Communications" (undergraduate honors thesis, Colorado State University, 2015), 3.

23. The bishop Eusebius took this approach in the fourth century, when he described the priesthood and monastic living as "the perfect form of the Christian life," in contrast to "the more humble, more human [life that] permits men to . . . have minds for farming, for trade, and the other more secular interests as well as for religion. . . . A kind of secondary grade of piety is attributed to them." In other words, those in sacred vocations are prime citizens in God's kingdom, whereas the rest of us can, at best, become second-class Christians. See Eusebius (c. 260–c. 339), *Demonstration of the Gospel*; quoted in Darrow L. Miller, *LifeWork: A Biblical Theology for What You Do Every Day* (Seattle: YWAM Publishing, 2009).

24. Gordon T. Smith, *Courage and Calling: Embracing Your God-Given Potential* (Downers Grove, IL: IVP Books, 2011), 45–46.

25. Notice how Paul invokes the Trinity in these verses—"same Spirit . . . same Lord . . . same God." The three persons of the Trinity are distinct, yet are one: a perfect model of diversity and unity that our gifts reflect.

26. Frank Parsons, *Choosing a Vocation* (Boston: Houghton Mifflin, 1909), 5.

27. That is, people who fit their current job well are more satisfied with their work than are people who don't fit as well. This pattern holds at the occupation, organization, team, and direct-report levels. See Amy L. Kristof-Brown, Ryan D. Zimmerman, and Erin C. Johnson, "Consequences of Individuals' Fit at Work: A Meta-Analysis of Person-Job, Person-Organization, Person-Group, and Person-Supervisor Fit," *Personnel Psychology* 58 (2005), 281–342.

28. See, for example, Michael J. Breslin and Christopher A. Lewis, "Theoretical Models of the Nature of Prayer and Health: A Review," *Mental Health, Religion and Culture* 11, no. 1 (2008), 9–21.

29. Douglas J. Schuurman, *Vocation: Discerning Our Callings in Life* (Grand Rapids: Eerdmans, 2004), 54.

30. "97-Year-Old Dies Unaware of Being Violin Prodigy," *The Onion*, October 4, 2010, https://local.theonion.com/97-year-old-dies-unaware-of-being-violin-prodigy-1819571799. Reprinted with permission of the *Onion*. Copyright © 2010, by Onion, Inc.

31. Much of what follows borrows heavily from a helpful book by Kevin DeYoung that explores the notion of God's will as it applies to human decision-making: *Just Do Something: A Liberating Approach to Finding God's Will* (Chicago: Moody Publishers, 2009).

32. This introduces big questions about the problem of evil, which we do not tackle here. But as DeYoung states, "Every human lamentation and woe must look to the cross. For there we see the problem of evil 'answered'—not in some theoretical sense—but by pointing us to an all-powerful God who works all things for good. Shocking as it sounds, the most heinous act of evil and injustice ever perpetrated on the earth—the murder of the Son of God—took place according to God's gracious and predetermined will" (ibid., 20).

33. Ibid., 24.

34. U.S. Department of Labor, Bureau of Labor Statistics, "Number of Jobs, Labor Market Experience, and Earnings Growth: Results from a National Longitudinal Survey," press release, August 22, 2019, https://www.bls.gov/news.release/pdf/nlsoy.pdf.

CHAPTER 3

35. Ruth Haley Barton includes an appendix in her book *Pursuing God's Will Together* that describes the ancient practice of *lectio divina*, a discipline that involves reading a short passage of Scripture (usually no more than six to eight verses) several times very slowly, diving into the layers of meaning with the text more deeply with each subsequent reading.

The goal is for this process to help tear through the cognitive filters we hold that may otherwise cause us to overlook words or messages in the text we may not be aware we need. Barton, *Pursuing God's Will Together* (Downer's Grove, IL: InterVarsity Press, 2012).

36. Ibid.

37. Meta-analyses are goldmines of information, because they estimate overall effects across many dozens of studies.

38. Steven D. Brown and Nancy E. Ryan Krane, "Four (or Five) Sessions and a Cloud of Dust: Old Assumptions and New Observations about Career Counseling," in *Handbook of Counseling Psychology*, 3rd ed., ed. Steven D. Brown and Robert W. Lent (New York: Wiley, 2000), 195–226.

39. If you need help remembering these components, reorder them and use the acronym WIMSI.

40. A more recent meta-analysis led by Susan Whiston examined career decision self-efficacy (or confidence) as the outcome measure, whereas Brown and Ryan Krane focused on career maturity (i.e., a person's readiness for making developmentally relevant educational or vocational decisions). Because of its tremendous impact on the vocational psychology literature in the last couple of decades, I frame this chapter around Brown and Ryan Krane's study. But see also Susan C. Whiston, Li Yue, Nancy Goodrich Mitts, and Lauren Wright, "Effectiveness of Career Choice Interventions: A Meta-Analytic Replication and Extension," *Journal of Vocational Behavior* 100 (2017), 175–184.

41. James W. Pennebaker and Joshua M. Smyth, *Opening Up by Writing It Down: How Expressive Writing Improves Health and Eases Emotional Pain* (New York: Guildford, 2016).

42. Laura A. King, "The Health Benefits of Writing about Life Goals," *Personality and Social Psychology Bulletin* 27 (2001), 798–807.

43. Why does writing help? Autobiographical writing forces us to translate sometimes vague or not-yet-well-formed ideas about our lives into a coherent narrative. That requires giving it some structure and organization and visualizing it more clearly. Doing so can help us identify areas of experience that need further exploration and discovery, and it can also help map out a path forward, toward a promising destination. Once that destination is articulated, a person can evaluate it, modify it where necessary, and set goals that will assist in pursuing the desired outcome. The process may also be cathartic, a chance to express some pent-up emotion rooted in our concerns.

44. Bob Goff, *Multi-Careering: Do Work That Matters at Every Stage of Your Journey* (Grand Rapids: Zondervan, 2013).

45. SMARTER builds on the SMART acronym, which appears to have originated decades ago with George T. Doran, a consultant and former director of corporate planning for Washington Water Power Company (George T. Doran, "There's a S.M.A.R.T. Way to Write Management's Goals and Objectives," *Management Review* 70 [1981]: 35–36). The original five SMART principles evolved somewhat in light of advances in research on goal-setting, which was pioneered by psychologists Ed A. Locke and Gary P. Latham, *A Theory of Goal Setting and Task Performance* (Englewood Cliffs, NJ: Prentice-Hall, 1990). Expanding to SMARTER is my own invention; it adds a little complexity but better captures Locke and Latham's seminal work.

46. I mean, unless you've been training and have the trip booked already, obviously. Then it is merely an extremely challenging (but not totally unattainable) goal.

47. Unfortunately, it can be very difficult on the surface to tell the difference between a high-quality, scientifically sound assessment and one that looks flashy but has no scientific basis. How can you discern between the two? The key lies in evaluating how well the developers of an instrument make efforts to establish the reliability and validity of its scores. *Reliability* refers to the extent to which scores provide consistent information, free from random error. *Validity* is a bit broader; it refers to the extent to which scores on an assessment meet the claims that the developer of the assessment makes for them. There are different types of reliability and validity, and establishing evidence of each type is expensive and labor-intensive for assessment developers. For that reason, it is not always done well, if it is even done at all, but publishers of assessments with scientific support usually do a good job of making the evidence of this support available.

48. Social cognitive career theory most directly addresses the role of modeling as a core influence on self-efficacy. See, for example, Robert W. Lent, "A Social Cognitive View of Career Development and Counseling," in *Career Development and Counseling: Putting Theory and Research to Work*, ed. Steven D. Brown and Robert W. Lent (New York: Wiley, 2005), 101–127.

49. Bryan J. Dik and Michael F. Steger, "Randomized Trial of a Calling-Infused Career Workshop Incorporating Counselor Self-Disclosure," *Journal of Vocational Behavior* 73 (2008), 203–211.

50. See, for example, Consuelo Arbona, "The Development of Academic Achievement in School-Aged Children: Precursors to Career Development," in *Handbook of Counseling Psychology*, ed. Steven D. Brown and Robert W. Lent (Hoboken, NJ: Wiley, 2000), 270–309.

CHAPTER 4

51. Check out 1 Corinthians 12, which we reviewed in chapter 2, as well as Romans 12:4–8; Ephesians 4:7–16; and 1 Peter 4:10–11.

52. W. Bruce Walsh, "What We Know and Need to Know: A Few Comments," in *Vocational Interests: Meaning, Measurement and Counseling Use*, ed. Mark L. Savickas and Arnold. R. Spokane (Palo Alto, CA: Davies-Black, 1999), 371–382.

53. If seeing this name associated with interests rings a bell, it is probably because Strong created an assessment instrument to measure interests, predecessor to the famous inventory that still bears his name: the Strong Interest Inventory.

54. E. K. Strong Jr., *Vocational Interests of Men and Women* (Palo Alto, CA: Stanford University Press, 1943), 17.

55. More recent research has also found remarkable continuity (on average) in people's interests over time, even across intervals longer than thirty years. See K. S. Douglas Low, Mijung Yoon, Brent W. Roberts, and James Rounds, "The Stability of Interests from Early Adolescence to Middle Adulthood: A Quantitative Review of Longitudinal Studies," *Psychological Bulletin* 131 (2005), 713–737.

56. Phillip L. Ackerman and Eric D. Heggestad, "Intelligence, Personality, and Interests: Evidence for Overlapping Traits," *Psychological Bulletin* 121 (1997), 239.

57. Holland's original statement of his theory can be found in John L. Holland, "A Theory of Vocational Choice," *Journal of Counseling Psychology* 6 (1959), 35–45. An update of the theory proposed late in his career can be found in John L. Holland, *Making Vocational Choices: A Theory of Vocational Personalities and Work Environments*, 3rd ed. (Odessa, FL: Psychological Assessment Resources, 1997).

58. I say "generally" because some people have profiles that suggest just one type might be the most accurate code—for example, someone with very high artistic interests and low-to-moderate interests in everything else. Early in my career I conducted a study that tried to assess whether using codes of various lengths (e.g., one, two, or three letters) made a difference in terms of predicting job satisfaction, compared to using three-letter codes regardless of the "shape" of people's profiles. The results suggested that there wasn't a meaningful difference (Bryan J. Dik, Ryan S. Hu, and Jo-Ida C. Hansen, "An Empirical Test of the Modified *C* Index and SII, O*NET, and DHOC Occupational Code Classifications," *Journal of Career Assessment* 15 [2007]: 279–300).

59. These constitute an updated version of the taxonomy that was developed

by University of Minnesota counseling psychologist René Dawis and his longtime collaborator, the late Lloyd Lofquist: *A Psychological Theory of Work Adjustment* (Minneapolis: University of Minnesota Press, 1984).

60. For decades, the best-supported model consisted of five superordinate traits known as the "Big Five." During the 1990s, research on the Big Five exploded, finding support in thousands of studies of people in diverse cultures and from all walks of life. (For an excellent overview, see Oliver P. John, Laura P. Naumann, and Christopher J. Soto, "Paradigm Shift to the Integrative Big Five Trait Taxonomy: History, Measurement, and Conceptual Issues," in *Handbook of Personality: Theory and Research*, ed. Oliver P. John, Richard W. Robins, and Lawrence A. Pervin [New York: Guilford, 2008], 114–158.) During the late 1990s, a pair of graduate students in Canada, Kibeom Lee and Michael Ashton, became curious about whether there was actually more to the story than these five super-ordinate traits. They recognized that computing power had advanced substantially since the time the Big Five first rose to prominence, so they began to conduct studies using a larger set of trait adjectives than had become common practice in personality research. When they did so, again across many countries, languages, and walks of life, they dis-covered a sixth factor. They called it Honesty/Humility, added it to the other five, and named this new framework using the acronym HEX-ACO. (See Kibeom Lee and Michael C. Ashton, *The H Factor of Personality* [Waterloo, ON: Wilfrid Laurier University Press, 2013].) As new research accumulated that consistently supported the HEXACO model, it gained traction and is increasingly recognized as the best current working model of the basic building blocks of personality.

61. Some people familiar with other personality models also bristle at cer-tain patterns of HEXACO scores that are not particularly positive—for example, low honesty-humility, low agreeableness, or low emotional stability (and perhaps low conscientiousness). Yet when people reflect on their experience in relationships with other people in their lives, it becomes readily apparent that those unpleasant combinations of traits are common. In my experience interpreting personality scores for peo-ple, those who score in these negative directions are rarely defensive about it. They quickly recognize that tendencies like wanting to break the rules, rapidly growing impatient, feeling easily stressed, or strug-gling to follow through with responsibilities are very familiar aspects of their experience in life. Even so, when thinking about career options, a good goal is to identify pathways that play to your strengths, even while working on your growth edges.

62. Comprehensive ability tests that do not rely on self-reporting are difficult to administer reliably in an online environment, which is why they
are not currently included in PathwayU. Instruments such as the Ability Profiler and the Highlands Ability Battery have strong evidence for
reliability and validity and are recommended, although they take hours
to complete. One online ability assessment that shows promise and is
worth checking out is YouScience (youscience.com).

CHAPTER 5

63. Here's another example: From time to time I lead workshops for organizations, usually to help evaluate how well their culture fosters a sense
of calling among employees. One of the first things I ask a group is how
many of them, when they think about work, feel like they have a calling.
Usually around half raise their hands. Then I ask those folks to describe
their calling for their coworkers. Almost none of them lead with their
job title. Instead, nearly all share about the broader themes their work
helps to accomplish. This is especially obvious among faculty and staff
at liberal arts colleges, the type of group I'm privileged to work with fre-
quently. None of these folks has ever described their calling as limited
to a specific job title, such as "to be a biology professor"—even though
many years of training may have gone into preparing for that path.
Rather, they say their calling is to help students develop their potential,
or to think critically and creatively about problems we face in the world,
or to create an environment in which people can learn, grow, and find
inspiration. A biology professor can do all of those things, but people in
other roles can, too.

64. The unpacking of this verse was heavily informed by a Tim Keller sermon that Sherman found inspiring, as she describes in the book.

65. Amy Sherman, *Kingdom Calling: Vocational Stewardship for the Common
Good* (Downers Grove, IL: IVP Books, 2011), 16.

66. Ibid., 17.

CHAPTER 6

67. Liu, Songqi, Jason L. Huang, and Mo Wang. "Effectiveness of Job Search
Interventions: A Meta-Analytic Review." *Psychological Bulletin 140* (2014),
1009–41.

68. Identifying just how many available positions occupy this so-called hidden job market is extremely difficult, but the best estimates (derived
from U.S. Bureau of Labor Statistics data) suggest that around 70 percent

of U.S. jobs are filled via networking, compared to 15 to 20 percent via job boards. Regardless of the precise numbers, the general principle that follows is eminently reasonable—in an environment in which employers strive to minimize risk in hiring, the more you can become a known quantity who impresses a hiring manager even prior to an interview, the better your odds of being hired.

69. This point and the sequence that follows is one of several in this section that were advanced by the late Dick Bolles in his classic book *What Color Is Your Parachute: A Practical Manual for Job-Hunters and Career Changers* (New York: Ten Speed Press, 2018).

70. Tom Jackson, *The Perfect Résumé: Today's Ultimate Job Search Tool* (New York: Broadway Books, 2004). Cited in Bolles, *What Color Is Your Parachute?*

71. I put it this way because research has questioned the effectiveness of relying on interviews in hiring (especially unstructured interviews), since interview performance is only weakly related to eventual job performance. See Frank L. Schmidt and John E. Hunter, "The Validity and Utility of Selection Methods in Personnel Psychology: Practical and Theoretical Implications of 85 Years of Research Findings," *Psychological Bulletin* 124 (1998), 262–274.

72. Stepane Côté, Alan M. Saks, and Jelena Zikic, "Trait Affect and Job Search Outcomes," *Journal of Vocational Behavior* 68 (2006), 233–252.

73. Self efficacy, outcome expectations, and goals are the three key variables used in social cognitive career theory, first articulated in this paper: Robert W. Lent, Steven D. Brown, and Gail Hackett, "Toward a Unifying Social Cognitive Theory of Career and Academic Interest, Choice, and Performance," *Journal of Vocational Behavior* 45 (1994), 79 122.

74. Ruth Kanfer, Connie R. Wanberg, and Tracy M. Kantrowitz, "Job Search and Employment: A Personality-Motivational Analysis and Meta-Analytic Review," *Journal of Applied Psychology* 86 (2001), 837–855.

75. Dov Eden and Arie Aviram, "Self-Efficacy Training to Speed Reemployment: Helping People to Help Themselves," *Journal of Applied Psychology* 78 (1993), 352–360.

76. Amiram Vinokur and Robert D. Caplan, "Attitudes and Social Support· Determinants of Job-Seeking Behavior and Well-Being among the Unemployed," *Journal of Applied Social Psychology* 17 (1987), 1007–1024.

77. John C. Rife and John R. Belcher, "Assisting Unemployed Older Workers to Become Reemployed: An Experimental Evaluation," *Research on Social Work Practice* 4 (1994), 3–13.

78. See, for example, Shelley E. Taylor, "Social Support: A Review," in *Handbook of Health Psychology*, ed. M. S. Friedman (New York: Oxford University Press, 2011), 189–214.

79. I say this confidently. It's a game of odds, and may require adjusting your strategy and broadening the scope of your search, but if you keep trying, your work will eventually pay off.

CHAPTER 7

80. Derek Thompson, "A World without Work," *The Atlantic*, July/August 2015, https://www.theatlantic.com/magazine/archive/2015/07/world-without-work/395294/; Andy Beckett, "Post-Work: The Radical Idea of a World Without Jobs," *The Guardian*, January 19, 2018, https://www.theguardian.com/news/2018/jan/19/post-work-the-radical-idea-of-a-world-without-jobs.

81. Much has been written about these and other changes, but I am following the lead of Philip Lorish in this chapter, who helpfully presented on these three "new normals" in his talk "The Disruption of Work: A Christian Take on the New Economy," presented at the 2018 Faith@Work Summit in Chicago.

82. Reid Hoffman, Ben Casnocha, and Chris Yeh, "Tours of Duty: The New Employer-Employee Compact," *Harvard Business Review* 91 (2013), 49–58.

83. Shep Hyken, "The Gig Economy Opens the Door for Employment Opportunities," July 29, 2018, https://www.forbes.com/sites/shephyken/2018/07/29/the-gig-economy-opens-the-door-for-employment-opportunities/#66f7d1837662.

84. Wayne Cascio and Ramiro Montealegre, "How Technology Is Changing Work and Organizations," *Annual Reviews of Organizational Psychology and Organizational Behavior* 3 (2016), 355.

85. Maddy Savage, "Thousands of Swedes Are Inserting Microchips under Their Skin," NPR, *All Things Considered*, October 22, 2018, https://www.npr.org/2018/10/22/658808705/thousands-of-swedes-are-inserting-microchips-under-their-skin.

86. HBO *VICE Special Reports*, "The Future of Work." April 20, 2019.

87. American Trucking Associations, "Reports, Trends, and Statistics," (no date), https://www.trucking.org/News_and_Information_Reports_Industry_Data.aspx.

88. Carl B. Frey and Michael A. Osborne, "The Future of Employment: How Susceptible Are Jobs to Computerization?" *Technological Forecasting and Social Change* 114 (2017), 254–280.

89. Carl B. Frey, Michael A. Osborne, Craig Holmes, Ebrahim Rahbari, Robert Garlick, George Friedlander, Graeme McDonald, Elizabeth Curmi,

Johanna Chua, Peter Chalif, and Martin Wilkie, "Technology at Work v2.0: The Future Is Not What It Used to Be," *Citi GPS:Global Perspectives and Solutions*, 2016.

90. Cascio and Montealegre, "How Technology is Changing Work and Organizations."

91. Evan Andrews, "Who Were the Luddites?" history.com, August 7, 2015 (updated June 26, 2019), https://www.history.com/news/who-were-the -luddites.

92. Mark L. Savickas and Erik J. Porfeli, "Career Adapt-Abilities Scale: Construction, Reliability, and Measurement," *Journal of Vocational Behavior* 80 (2012), 662.

93. Yet another meta-analysis: Cort W. Rudolph, Kristi N. Lavigne, and Hannes Zacher, "Career Adaptability: A Meta-Analysis of Relationships with Measures of Adaptivity, Adapting Responses, and Adaptation Results," *Journal of Vocational Behavior* 98 (2017), 17–34.

94. We have to be careful here, given that correlation does not equal causation. Most of the studies in Rudolph et al.'s meta-analysis are correlational, from which causal inferences cannot be made. It is of course possible that beneficial career development status boosts career adaptability rather than (or in addition to) the reverse. Third variables, such as well-being, maturity, intellectual ability, or social support may also promote both career adaptability and beneficial career development simultaneously. But evidence from experimental designs (e.g., Melanie Ohme and Hannes Zacher, "Job Performance Ratings: The Relative Importance of Mental Ability, Conscientiousness, and Career Adaptability," *Journal of Vocational Behavior* 87 [2015], 161–170) and longitudinal designs in which people are followed over time (e.g., Hannes Zacher, "Individual Difference Predictors of Change in Career Adaptability over Time," *Journal of Vocational Behavior* 84 [2014], 188–198) lend support for the conclusion that career adaptability leads to positive outcomes, so I feel confident in making the causal inference here.

95. To be clear, these kinds of structural barriers are a result of structural sin within human society, and need to be eradicated. My goal here is not to simply accept these barriers with a shrug, but rather to acknowledge their reality and assist individuals in forging a path despite them, even while also working to undo them.

96. Deborah G. Betsworth and Jo-Ida C. Hansen, "The Categorization of Serendipitous Career Development Events," *Journal of Career Assessment* 4 (1996), 91–98.

97. David Kern, "Leaning to Look: Alissa Wilkinson on Eliminating Ego,

Setting Aside Taste, and Pushing Past the Obvious," *FORMA* 6 (2017), 9–11.

98. Ibid.

99. This is academic-speak for serving as an adjunct faculty member, an arrangement in which a university instructor is paid on a per-course basis.

100. Kevin Brown and Steven McMullen, "How to Find Hope in the Human-less Economy," *Christianity Today*, June 21, 2017, https://www.christian itytoday.com/ct/2017/july-august/how-to-have-hope-in-humanless-econ omy.html.

101. Tom Simonite, "Robots Will Take Jobs from Men, the Young, and Minorities," *Wired*, January 24, 2019, https://www.wired.com/story/robots-will -take-jobs-from-men-young-minorities/.

102. Many churches already help address employment needs within their local communities by hosting networking events, job search workshops, and mentoring programs. For example, Roswell United Methodist Church in Roswell, Georgia, offers an impressive breadth of job readiness workshops and coaching, all focused on helping participants find work while restoring their confidence in the creative and redemptive service they can offer the world, using their God-given gifts (https:// workingnation.com/im-a-believer/). Parachurch organizations like Jobs for Life (https://jobsforlife.org/) and Crossroads Career (https://cross roadscareer.org/) support churches in offering career coaching programs as an outreach ministry in their communities. Others, like Made to Flourish (https://madetoflourish.org) or the Denver Institute for Faith and Work near my community in Colorado, provide educational resources and experiences designed to equip Christians to think theologically, embrace relationships, create good work, seek deep spiritual health, and serve others sacrificially (https://denverinstitute.org/guid ing-principles/). At their best, such efforts do more than offer respite from a difficult world of work. They invite people to orient their lives to God's broader story of creation, fall, redemption, and renewal.

103. James E. Bessen, "How Computer Automation Affects Occupations: Technology, Jobs, and Skills," *Boston University School of Law, Law and Economics Research Paper* (2016), 15–49; Cascio and Montealegre, "How Technology Is Changing Work and Organizations"; Sarah Kessler, "The Optimist's Guide to the Robot Apocalypse," *Quartz*, March 9, 2017, https://qz.com/904285/; James Surowiecki, "The Great Tech Panic: Robots Won't Take All Our Jobs," *Wired*, September 2017, https://www .wired.com/2017/08/robots-will-not-take-your-job/.

104. Brown and McMullen, "How to Find Hope in the Humanless Economy."

CHAPTER 8

105. To be clear, the statues were beheaded, not the kings.
106. N. T. Wright, *Surprised by Hope: Rethinking Heaven, the Resurrection, and the Mission of the Church* (New York: HarperOne, 2008), 209.
107. Ibid., 210.
108. In fact, the varying resources given to the workers in the parable convey that our responsibilities for stewardship are proportional to the magnitude of the gifts with which we've been blessed. This insight, and those in the preceding paragraph, were drawn from a sermon on this text delivered by my father, Jack B. Dik, at Georgetown Christian Reformed Church, "Gold, Shovels, and Holes," Hudsonville, Michigan, August 23, 2015.
109. This point is emphasized by Tom Nelson in his book *Work Matters: Connecting Sunday Worship to Monday Work* (Wheaton, IL: Crossway, 2011).
110. Ibid., 75.
111. Wright, *Surprised by Hope*, 208.
112. This is a retelling of Wolter's analogy of an architect who provides recorded instructions to help an incompetent builder make sense of blueprints. I prefer comparing people to students who are learning rather than to incompetent builders who should know better, but both comparisons probably fit. See Albert M. Wolters, *Creation Regained: Biblical Basics for Reformational Worldview*, 2nd ed. (Grand Rapids: Eerdmans, 2005).
113. It also requires pushing past the status quo for many in the faith and work conversation today, who still adhere to the Two-Act Story thinking exhibited at that Fusing Faith and Life conference in chapter 1. Amy Sherman and colleagues recently examined the vision and planned events and activities for fifteen prominent "marketplace ministry" organizations and found that for twelve of them, their efforts focused almost exclusively on witnessing to coworkers, establishing Bible studies and prayer times, and promoting personal discipleship through evangelism. *None* of the fifteen organizations examined by Sherman's team appeared to deeply explore the impact of the gospel on the work itself, or to promote a fully integrative approach to navigating faith and work. See Amy Sherman, *Kingdom Calling: Vocational Stewardship for the Common Good* (Downers Grove, IL: IVP Books, 2011).
114. See http://christynelsonart.com/.
115. See http://www.rachelsussman.com/sidewalk-kintsukuroi.

116. I had the honor of serving on Christy's MFA committee. These words are from Christy Nelson, *Forms of Transformation* (master's thesis, Colorado State University, 2019), 15.
117. Wright, *Surprised by Hope*, 207–208.
118. These three components of meaning originated with Frank Martela and Michael F. Steger, "The Three Meanings of Meaning in Life: Distinguishing Coherence, Purpose, and Significance," *Journal of Positive Psychology* 5 (2016), 531–545.

Appendix

119. Mihran Vardanyan, Roberto Trotta, and Joseph Silk, "Applications of Bayesian Model Averaging to the Curvature and Size of the Universe," *Monthly Notices of the Royal Astronomical Society* 413 (2001), L91-L95.
120. Christopher J. Conselice, Aaron Wilkinson, Kenneth Duncan, and Alice Mortlock, "The Evolution of Galaxy Number Density at Z< 8 and Its Implications," *Astrophysical Journal* 830 (2016), 83.
121. Sten Odenwald, "Counting the Stars in the Milky Way," *Huffington Post*, March 17, 2014; updated December 6, 2017, https://www.huffingtonpost.com/entry/number-of-stars-in-the-milky-way_b_4976030.html.
122. "Small Miracles: Harnessing Nanotechnology," *Terra: Inspired Stories from the Edge of Science*, Oregon State University, February 1, 2007, http://terra.oregonstate.edu/2007/02/small-miracles/.
123. And that's only the number that have been named and cataloged; there are as many as 30 million different species in total. See Smithsonian Institution, "Numbers of Insects (Species and Individuals)," 2017, https://www.si.edu/spotlight/buginfo/bugnos.
124. This is not to say that the Reformation's *sola scriptura* (Scripture alone) principle—the teaching that the Bible is sufficient as our supreme authority for all spiritual matters—is compromised when we strive to learn about God from both his creation and his Word. The two are in many ways different; the "book" of creation does not tell us about the message of sin and grace, for example. But they are clearly related. Al Wolters appeals to John Calvin in referring to Scripture as the spectacles that provide clarity to our otherwise obscured understanding of God. In other words, we gain a clearer sense of "creational normativity" when we understand it in light of Scripture. See Albert M. Wolters, *Creation Regained: Biblical Basics for Reformational Worldview*, 2nd ed. (Grand Rapids: Eerdmans, 2005).
125. Richard L. Pratt, *Designed for Dignity: What God Has Made It Possible for You to Be* (Phillipsburg, NJ: P&R Publishing, 1993), 20–21. Cited by H.

Whelchel, *How Then Shall We Work?* (McLean, VA: Institute for Faith, Work, and Economics, 2012).

126. Cornelius Plantinga Jr., *Engaging God's World: A Reformed Vision of Faith, Learning, and Living* (Grand Rapids: Eerdmans, 2002), 31.

127. The total depravity doctrine teaches that, because of the fall, humans are slaves to sin; our fallen nature makes us incapable of choosing to follow God, refraining from evil, or accepting the gift of salvation unless God's grace moves within us, enabling us to do so.

128. Albert M. Wolters, *Creation Regained: Biblical Basics for a Reformational Worldview*, 2nd ed. (Grand Rapids: Eerdmans, 2005), 44.

129. This is explored in depth in another of Plantinga's books: Cornelius Plantinga Jr., *Not the Way It's Supposed to Be: A Breviary of Sin* (Grand Rapids: Eerdmans, 1996).

130. Wolters, *Creation Regained*, 46.

131. Plantinga, *Engaging God's World*, 73.

132. Ibid., 77–78.

133. "Therefore, God elevated him to the place of highest honor and gave him the name above all other names, that at the name of Jesus every knee should bow, in heaven and on earth and under the earth, and every tongue confess that Jesus Christ is Lord, to the glory of God the Father" (Philippians 2:9–11).

134. Amy Sherman, *Kingdom Calling: Vocational Stewardship for the Common Good* (Downers Grove, IL: IVP Books, 2011), 79.

135. Wolters, *Creation Regained*, 58.

136. Ibid., 60.

137. Sherman, *Kingdom Calling*, 256.

138. Richard Middleton provides a detailed, multilayered analysis of this passage, drawing the same conclusion—the transformation and redemption of the world (see *A New Heaven and a New Earth: Reclaiming Biblical Eschatology* [Grand Rapids: Baker Academic, 2014]).

139. "Radically healed" is how N. T. Wright describes it: "The transition from the present world to the new one would be a matter not of destruction of the present space-time universe but of its radical healing" (*Surprised by Hope: Rethinking Heaven, the Resurrection, and the Mission of the Church* [New York: HarperOne, 2008], 122).

Index